ROLLER RINK
STARLIGHT

ROLLER RINK STARLIGHT

A MEMOIR

WILLIAM HART

EPIGRAPH BOOKS
RHINEBECK, NEW YORK

Paperback ISBN 978-1-951937-78-2
eBook ISBN 978-1-951937-79-9

Library of Congress Control Number 2020922445

Book design by Colin Rolfe
Author photo by Carolyn Isaak

Epigraph Books
22 East Market Street, Suite 304
Rhinebeck, NY 12572
(845) 876-4861

In memory of the Alaskan Roller Rink and its speed skaters

PREFACE

B Y calling this book a memoir I'm saying it is a factual account constructed from my memories. It's a story I lived between ages fourteen and eighteen, but it's not my story alone. In telling it I've incorporated scenes from the lives of other people, some of whom might have preferred to remain unmentioned. A memoir can invade privacy and reopen old wounds, and that's why it may require justification, as I believe this one does.

During adolescence I became a roller speed skater on a highly successful coed racing team representing my local rink. In skater society I received most of my early lessons in athletic competition, girls, and romance. My teammates of both sexes came from every economic class in our city and all five school districts, providing a fertile milieu for my growth as a person. So memorable were my rink years that after I became a writer they were what I most wanted to write about, though it took decades to figure out how. Early attempts to tell my story were fiction, and all were abandoned because I couldn't bring the characters to life. More recently I decided to present the people and events just as I remember them, without fictional embellishment, resulting in this book. Aside from my need to relate these experiences, there may be historical value in my insider's portrait of a beloved American institution highly in tune with its times. The public roller rink I portray is the Alaskan in Wichita, Kansas, circa 1960.

No memoir is completely true, of course, nor are memories always accurate. Some conversations here are reconstructed from the parts I recall, and in places I've altered time sequence. To protect feelings and reputations I've changed the names and personal data of about half the cast. I apologize to anyone hurt or offended by my portrayals. I tried to give what I believe I owe most—my unvarnished recollections told with minimal bias.

ONE

GRETCHEN sat behind me in seventh grade math, placing her in the last row of desks, the row teachers recognize as a hangout for the disaffected. From the first day she distracted me by talking to the back of my head. Not that I minded. Gretchen could be very entertaining. She was a skinny twelve-year-old with a bright, winning face and a smile a bit manic in its intensity. She had a taste for sardonic humor and a gift for mockery. Dropping her head down behind mine so our teacher couldn't see her mouth moving, she would in a low voice heap derision on her victim, usually our teacher.

Mr. Benjamin was a kind, inoffensive man who had apparently dedicated his life to the utopian dream of basic math literacy for all. His only fault was his profound squareness. For instance, he liked to tell stories with morals aimed straight at us. The one I remember best happened while he was stationed in Finland with his army unit after WWII. He and his Finnish fiancée maintained their virginities on her family's farm for a whole week, right up to their wedding night, when they enjoyed a consummation more meaningful because it was pure.

I heard a muffled explosion of air behind me followed by suppressed giggles. "What a load! I bet he screwed her in the sauna."

Our teacher's starry-eyed devotion to the high road seemed to provoke Gretchen.

We shared that class with a girl who dressed like a fourth grader and carried a big notebook with the head of a horse embossed on its plastic cover. Gretchen referred to this timid personality as Horsey Girl and speculated about whether our slow-maturing classmate hosted teas for her dolls and slept with her stuffed animals. Gretchen never bullied the object of her scorn, never spoke to her that I saw, yet ridiculed her with a puzzling ferocity. Did she hate Horsey Girl for refusing to grow up—or for her innocence?

As Gretchen and I became friends she talked less about others and more about herself, regaling me with her exploits. One day she asked the back of my head if I'd ever had sex. When I admitted I hadn't, she said she had and proceeded to tell about her first time. She and a boy in her sixth-grade class snuck back into the school during recess and did it standing up in their cloakroom. She'd liked it. She poked me in the back and laughed. "You should try it sometime." Was she putting me on? I wasn't sure, but she definitely got my attention. Sex with Gretchen in a cloakroom joined the stock of fantasies I called upon in bed at night while saying my prayers to Venus.

Having learned I was interested in her personal life, Gretchen kept me posted. Once she told about the night before, when she'd played strip poker with three ninth graders in a basement bedroom. Another time she reported entertaining four East High guys in a parked car. Her X-rated vignettes were delivered with a big grin, making me think she was trying to shock me—yet I believed her. Her stories held together and the details were convincing. She opened my mind to what was possible sexually for a seventh grader.

Next she began coming on to me. The first time was the day Mr. Benjamin called us to his desk so we could view our midterm test scores in his gradebook. I was standing, waiting my turn, when someone stepped behind me and leaned into my back. It was Gretchen. I realized what I was feeling were the two little peaks that showed through her sweater when she sat up straight. I liked what she was doing. I held still so she could press herself against me any way she pleased. I was intrigued that her breasts felt soft and firm at the same time. When I glanced back at her she grinned.

Gretchen had a big pink eraser with nicely rounded edges that rubbed out pencil marks like nobody's business and smelled lovely while doing it. I got in the habit of borrowing it when I had a lot to erase. It was especially useful on tests because it helped me avoid ripped pages. It helped her on tests too. If she needed to check an answer, we communicated by eraser mail.

"Reach back," Gretchen whispered one day. I did and felt her eraser being pressed into my palm. I brought it up and examined it. One side was blank but on the other side in bold block letters she'd penciled "POKE ME." Warm breath bathed the back of my neck as she delivered the same message in its most vulgar form, using the throaty whisper of a woman dizzy with desire. I thought I could meet her request. I'd been soloing with confidence for more than a year. Certainly I was willing. What I couldn't figure out was *where* to do it. Unlike Gretchen's high-school guys I didn't have a car, and I was too young to rent a motel room. The city parks were out because it was winter. Then it dawned on me that Gretchen, with her greater experience, probably knew exactly where to go. I turned the eraser over to its blank side, licked my pencil lead and printed, "Okay. Where?" When Gretchen read my response, muffled laughter burst out behind me. I couldn't understand what was funny.

On the last day of school each semester our teachers computed our grades and recorded them on our report cards. We could do as we liked if we stayed quiet and in our seats. I was doodling to kill time in math when the silence was broken by a ninth grader joining us. His smile was defiant. Randy Santeer had a rep for causing trouble, and I figured he'd been sent to us so Mr. Benjamin could put a lid on him. Our math teacher was also Roosevelt's vice principal.

Randy slid into a desk in the back row, placing him directly across the room from Gretchen. I heard a snicker behind me and turned to find the two eyeing each other lecherously, making clear the nature of their relationship. Gretchen mouthed silently the same invitation she'd made to me—I could see the words moving on her lips—while Randy grinned at her with a leer so lustful it shocked me. I glanced at Mr. Benjamin. His fountain pen was suspended in midair as he watched the hardcore flirts with deep concern. I thought he was going to say something to them but he didn't. When they noticed him watching, their communion ended. Soon our teacher was handing out grade reports and then the bell was ringing. Math being our last class of the day, we poured through the door into Christmas vacation.

In January Gretchen returned to our class a week late, and she was not the same Gretchen. Her overly bright smile was gone and so was her cockiness. Her mockery was gone, in its place a new respect for Mr. Benjamin and for others, even Horsey Girl. In one long, last monologue delivered to the back of my head she explained that after our last class our teacher had hauled Randy and her into his office, where he got them to divulge what they'd been up to. "He made me tell him the names of everybody who screwed me." There were around fifteen boys, all students at our intermediate or at East High next door. Gretchen and the guys had to attend conferences accompanied by their parents where an officer from the Wichita PD spelled out the laws and penalties attaching to sex with a minor. All involved were suspended from school for a week. I wondered how Gretchen's parents reacted to the news of her escapades, but she didn't go into that and I didn't pry.

It seemed Gretchen liked the way things turned out. She was more relaxed after that—and much quieter. For the rest of the school year she left me alone. I was glad for her because I thought she'd been headed in the wrong direction. Yet I missed the old Gretchen. I missed her high spirits and the scathing humor that sometimes nailed it. Those fun qualities had been rooted out along with her premature sexuality.

The following year, eighth grade, my honors classes began. The student taking Gretchen's place at the desk behind me in math was my friend Bob Nickel, someone eager to compete with me almost to the death in any contest two young males could devise. Bob would become valedictorian at our high school of four thousand, ace his way through Stanford, graduate first in his medical school class at the University of California, then blossom into an internationally respected pediatrician. And he wasn't the only fierce competitor in that class. Struggling to pre-vail in our academic pressure cooker, we cranked up the heat on everyone to a high boil. Sadly, a bureaucratic oversight had neutralized our tried and true pressure release. Honors classes back then, especially in the sciences and math, were packed with guys and sprinkled with girls—a poor way for either sex to thrive, as we now know. For us sharp-elbowed males it meant we went largely without the softer, more fragrant buffers that had saved us from ourselves in earlier years.

These changes at school altered my social life—and to some extent my personality. As I vied with bright, ambitious minds in all my courses, my innate antisocial tendencies received too much nourishment, warping me into a nerd. My native introver-sion deepened, boosting my allergy to group activities. In time I could click socially only when hanging with nerd buddies who shared my afflictions. We walked to school in a brain trust of four or five, convened frequently around a basketball or football, shared parent-free zones of each other's homes—hangouts raunchy with sarcasm and mocking laughter. Safe in our brotherhood of outsiders, we rejected the dumbed-down, conventional world where schoolmates our age threw parties and organized events and—we imagined—enjoyed interactions so smooth that girls and guys paired up painlessly.

My life was okay I guess, but I really missed the stimulating variety of girls that had brightened my previous schooldays. I'd become a romantic trapped in a closet, lacking what I wanted most—a girlfriend. Naturally I made her up. Attractive females I saw in school hallways, on TV, and in my dreams became my one and only in a long series of intoxicating fantasies, allowing me to romance around the clock. When a teacher droned, my darling floated down to share my desk and we made out. After dinner, her devastating face peeked out at me from a parka in *The Alaskans*, a television series featuring almost-too-blonde Dorothy Provine. At night, the soft rock ballads flowing from the radio beside my bed brought her to me on waves of passion, racking my heart just right. And to be sure we got lucky between my sheets, driven by a hard rock beat. The only place I didn't encounter her was in reality, and that's because the barren nerd world where I hum-drummed through my days offered more chance of bumping into a unicorn than a living, breathing fox.

Without realizing it, I was banishing myself from the human mating pool when my little brother accidentally rescued me by introducing me to roller speed skating. Roller skating and the people who did it steered me away from the bleak future I was headed toward and into one more in line with my natural bent.

TWO

ROTHER John, three years younger, has a knack for coming up with superior ideas though he often feels no need to let me in on them. He began visiting our local roller rink before I knew it existed. I learned of it not from him but from the sudden appearance of his racing skates standing proud among the galoshes under the coatrack in our rec room. The beautiful hand-crafted, leather-booted quads had bigger wheels in back than in front, like hotrods, and were surprisingly light.

A week or so later, above the skates I found a gold satin jacket glowing boldly among my family's otherwise drab outerwear. A sizzling black stripe ran down either sleeve, and on the rear panel black cursive lettering spelled out "Alaskan Speed Club." The jacket, perfect for a minor superhero, was too flashy for me, but the skates were to die for. I pictured them on my feet and me jetting down the pike.

I remembered sidewalk skating with the metal clamp-ons I got for Christmas in fifth grade. On days when the concrete was free of snow and ice, I shoved into high gear and clackity-clacked around the four sidewalks of the block cattycorner to ours, filling the day sleepers with thoughts of mayhem. Fueled by my inborn hyperactivity and a pound or two of holiday sugar, I trained with devotion on my quarter-mile track until I could spring up from my seat in front of the television and do a hot lap during a commercial break. Back then skating had been a kick, and now that I was a sprinter on my junior high track team I thought I might have the stuff to be a skate racer. One evening, I tagged along as the parents drove John to a public session at the rink.

A mile west of our home, in an older residential neighborhood turning inner city, the Alaskan Roller Rink loomed above the frame houses and apartments surrounding it like a three-story, humpbacked, lime-green leviathan. It was one of the largest roller rinks in the United States, then or ever, built during the 1920s as a public *ice* skating arena. In the 1930s, seating was expanded to fifteen hundred to accommodate crowds for pro hockey in the NHL. In 1954, probably for economic reasons, the Alaskan was converted from ice to a roller rink.

My brother and I paid the fifty-cent admission at a ticket window below a marquee, then entered the building foyer, where I rented skates for fifteen cents at a window in the wall. We walked by the concession area with its grill and long Formica serving counter and into the rink proper, where forty or fifty skaters circled the floor. The building interior was so large that three modern cinderblock rinks would fit easily inside its foundation, nine or so within its cavernous volume. The skating surface was a vast expanse of well-maintained tongue-and-groove maple hardwood flooring surrounded on three sides by a yard-high wood barrier that kept speeding bodies from flying into the lower spectator sections. Behind the barrier, solid wood bleachers ascended thirty feet to the base of walls supporting the domed roof. From the center of the roof hung a big globe covered in mirrors that we would begin calling a "disco ball" in the 1970s, but which had been around for at least eighty years before, known boringly as a "mirror ball." Even with its mundane name, it packed magic. During couples skates, with the floor lights extinguished, the thousand reflective surfaces of the rotating sphere probed the far reaches of the arena with flying beams of light, brushing everyone and everything with its alchemy.

John and I sat on a bench immediately behind the wooden barrier and changed into our skates. We rolled along the aisle below the bleachers, then descended a ramp to the floor where we merged with the crowd moving counterclockwise. The glide of my rented plastic wheels on maple was nearly frictionless—nirvana for a sidewalk skater. We'd joined a "free skate," one of many during any session. There would also be six to eight skates for couples and four for those who wanted to race—two Men Onlys and two Ladies Onlys. During the fast skates up-tempo numbers rocked the joint at high volume, while during the pairs skates slow and moody love tunes blared equally loud, swelling the building with passion. The last skate of the night was always for couples.

During my first Men Only I channeled my sidewalk skater's alternating leg thrust and found it worked okay on the straight-aways where others were doing the same. But around the turns I lost ground quickly to skaters scissoring their legs in a style unknown on sidewalks. As I tried to fathom this mysterious technique, five or six of the best racers formed a tight line and streamed around the oval like a runaway train, slicing through the rest of us with casual arrogance. Alaskan Speed Club jackets flapped on several backs. This clannish performance bugged me, yet I had to admire the art of it, especially when they one after another leaned into a turn and went low—some touching the floor with their fingertips—then drove into the next straightaway on scissoring legs.

Half an hour later Ladies Only was announced and Del Shannon's "Runaway" began firing up the female racers. My brother and I watched from the bench behind the rail where we'd laced up our skates, a bench rapidly becoming "ours" by virtue of our occupying posteriors. It would be our bench for years. The ladies (age nine or so to around twenty) streaked by us as they accelerated out of a turn, demonstrating the scissoring legs I needed to make me a competitive racer. I saw it was a matter of placing the right skate inside the left repeatedly around the curve, changing directions by increments while pushing forward.

Most of the legs in my study were lean and shapely, probably because they were better exercised than most female legs in that late fifties heyday of the automobile. I checked out the rest of each girl, learning that many were pretty, though some were too old for me and some too young. Then I saw the prettiest one close to me in age, a blonde with a radiant face and curvy body. She was among the fastest skaters though her style was calm and unhurried. When she drove through the turn, leaning forward and swinging her arms, her blouse pulled tight against her womanly chest, yet it was her serene face that drew my eyes. Smiling the barest of smiles she seemed above it all. I knew she had to be on the speed club. I asked my brother who she was.

For the rest of the session I tried to keep track of Gloria Linsey. I saw her during the free skates with her girlfriends, some in speed-club jackets. When couples rolled through the dark I looked for her, afraid I'd see her, but I didn't. Under the flashing mirror ball her highly reflective hair would have been a giveaway. During a free skate late in the session Gloria was joined by another blonde who looked like a younger sister and they circled the floor having a serious talk. The younger girl seemed to be filling Gloria in on something. After that I lost track of both girls and didn't see them again that night. As my fact-finding mission drew to a close, I knew I'd return to the Alaskan. I was hooked.

THREE

began visiting the rink several nights a week, usually walking there then riding home on the parental shuttle with my brother. Soon I owned a pair of racing skates and was paying speed club dues, both funded by the folks. Our parents typically financed any activity John or I took up that they approved of. They must have viewed roller skating as a way to get us off our butts and away from the TV.

I loved speed skating even before I could speed skate adequately. I never missed team practice and raced in every Men Only like a boy on fire. After Saturday practice and before the night session I snuck onto the floor and blazed around the oval alone until a push broom began pumping debris at me. Routinely I tested my upper limits, so I went down a lot, collecting floor burns on my arms and elbows and spraining my right thumb so many times it developed a thick bulb of cartilage at its base. Once I sprained my coccyx. You don't even know you have a coccyx until you sprain it, then you know every time you sit down.

As I got faster my falls became more violent and more spectacular. They often concluded with me sliding across the floor on my hip and slamming into the wood barrier. Fortunately, the Alaskan's huge floor was forgiving, as was its soft-wood barrier sealed in rubberized paint, so I could always hop up and rejoin the action. My devotion to my new sport boosted my learning curve and in a few months I mastered basic racing mechanics. I could scissor out of turns with power and was refining my start into an advantage. My individual style was emerging, one that drew on my long stride as a sprinter. I could beat some of the guys on the club in my age group.

Although I was now Gloria Linsey's teammate, she still didn't know I existed. Meanwhile I was too aware of her. I watched her as much as I could without giving away the towering crush I'd foolishly developed on someone who stared right through me. At practice I learned she was by far the youngest member of our A-team Ladies Relay. This meant she was *really* fast and that I'd have to become one of the best racers on the club to have a chance with her. Good, I thought. More motivation. The girl I'd guessed was Gloria's younger sister actually was, and her name was Katy. They had a brother even younger named Greg, and he and my brother, in the same grade at different schools, were already buddies.

I was struck by the togetherness of the three Linseys. They seemed a little family unto themselves, well-functioning and supportive. Gloria took the mother role and her siblings looked up to her and let her guide them. I never saw Katy or Greg defy big sister or even seriously question her. She in turn led gently and with intelligence. I think Gloria was reasonably happy, yet her placid, thoughtful face seemed touched by sadness. Later I wondered if her muted smile, reminiscent of the Mona Lisa's, came from knowing too much too soon.

In June, although my brother and I had been racing for only a few months, we signed up to compete in our age divisions at the 1959 RSROA Regional Championships in Greeley, Colorado. We rode west to the Rocky Mountains with Alan Edwards, a younger teammate, while his father drove. Mr. Edwards let us boys share a motel room unsupervised, leading to marathon pillow fights and greasy pig-outs supplied by the McDonald's across the street. For lunch one day we shared ten orders of French fries drenched in ketchup for a buck plus tax.

I'd hoped to see Gloria in Greeley but it didn't happen. I did run into her younger sister after my quarter mile final. I was leaving the rink carrying my skates as Katy entered with her skate case. I held the door for her and she thanked me. Then she stopped and asked, "How are your races going?" I was surprised because she'd never spoken to me before. I told her I'd just placed fourth in my quarter-mile final, adding, "Two guys ahead of me fell down." She smiled and said I was "doing real good" considering how long I'd been racing. That was our entire exchange yet I was thrilled. Katy Linsey knew who I was! If she knew, maybe her sister did too.

A month later the members of our speed club who'd qualified at regionals for the RSROA national championships traveled by train to Chicago. Their absence sucked the spirit from several sessions as the rest of us tried to pretend we didn't need them. Being bored at the Alaskan was a new experience for me, sad and demoralizing.

I awoke one morning to the faint drone of the television downstairs in the rec room. I descended to find my little brother watching the Wichita morning talk show emceed by our biggest local TV celebrity, John Froome. Froome was interviewing the three Linseys. Greg had won his age division in Chicago, Katy had placed second in hers, and Gloria had skated on the winning ladies relay. Mr. Froome mentioned during his patter that the Alaskan Speed Club had captured eight national titles, more than any other team.

The Linseys were likely chosen to represent our club not only because they won medals. They were a telegenic well-matched set, three attractive blue-eyed blonds with the same last name. The girls seemed a little intimidated by the cameras but eleven-year-old Greg more than held his own with a series of inappropriate grins, clearly communicating what he thought of the whole affair.

I was thinking how great to be a national champion with a trophy and everyone's respect. The victories of the Linseys and my other teammates gave me hope. If I wanted to win a national title, it looked like I'd found the right speed club.

At the rink later that week I was watching the start of a couples skate when a certain affectionate pair caught my eye. It was common for lovers to drape themselves all over one another during the dark skates but these two hadn't stopped there. They were so thoroughly entwined and so close to the floor they suggested paramours in a bed on wheels as they slowly inched past me through the shadows. An open speed club jacket lay over them, concealing the position of their bodies as well as their doings. Between them and the floor I saw three skates and a dragging sleeve. Their mode of forward propulsion was anyone's guess.

The last strains of a billowing love song died in the speakers and the house lights came up as the rolling mound of together-ness rose from the floor, shedding the golden cocoon. A man in his early 20s emerged with a mid-teen girl. The man was hand-some and well-built and wore perfectly fitting blue jeans and a sport shirt with its short sleeves rolled up two turns on his tan, sculpted biceps. The girl looked and dressed exactly like Gloria Linsey, though I didn't want to believe it was. With my fantasies toppling inside me like glass skyscrapers I watched the pair coast by me again, upright but still in one another's arms, eyes only for each other, indisputably in love. It was Gloria for sure. *But who was the crib robber and where the hell had he come from?!*

An hour later I was glumly nursing my wounds when the lights faded and the DJ announced the couples skate created with shy guys like me in mind—Ladies Choice. I watched as Gloria and her man rolled onto the floor and began contorting them-selves into their low-slung love nest. It was painful to witness but apparently I needed to see every bit of it.

Then someone skated swiftly across the floor and stopped

against the rail directly in front of me. In the star-spangled twi-light I made out the blonde bangs and uncertain eyes of Gloria's sister Katy. "Wanna skate?" she asked. After weighing my options for approximately one second, I stood up, stepped over the rail onto the floor and took her hand. We joined the other couples and rolled hand in hand without speaking. I was afraid of saying the wrong thing and probably she was too. We both knew she'd just declared an interest in me, and now I had to decide whether I was interested in her.

I'd been so focused on Gloria I hadn't paid much attention to her sister. Now that I did, I liked what I saw. The crown of her sun-bleached hair came level with my mouth and somehow that seemed just right. Her arm next to mine was nicely tapered and although she was a petite girl I felt unusual strength in her hand and wrist. She was less mature physically than her sister, but I could live with that. Katy's lithe, athletic body was, like my own, just beginning to fill out.

At the end of our skate she thanked me, and I thanked her, and we went our separate ways. I kept tabs on her though and when the next couples skate was announced I rolled to her and asked her to join me. This time we were smiling as we clasped hands and pushed off into the circling throng. We were now a couple. It was a poignant moment, I think for both of us. We didn't spoil it with words.

Later I thought back on this one of a kind night and was puz-zled. I'd entered the rink in love with Gloria and left falling for her sister. Did that make sense? It didn't, yet it felt right, so right I refused to question it. I now had a girlfriend, one of the best rac-ers on our team and cute enough to star in my fantasies. What's more, when Katy chose me for her boyfriend she lifted me from rink obscurity into her clan of elite skaters, making me a some-body, though a lesser one, as yet unproven. I was grateful—and a little uneasy. What had I done to deserve so much good luck?

FOUR

PARENTS of speed club members were a varied lot. On our team the children of millionaires rubbed shoulders with kids from the wrong side of the tracks. In one way however all rink parents were pretty much alike—they shared a laissez-faire attitude toward child rearing. Some parents used the rink as a low-rent babysitter so they could indulge in a kid-free life. Others turned to the Alaskan for child care while working multiple jobs. There were parents who bribed their youngsters with entertainments to keep them from whining and those who couldn't say no. My parents based their decision to let us hang out at the rink three or four nights a week on personal belief. They supported child liberation before most people knew it existed and gave my brother and me, from the time we were ten or so, maximum reasonable freedom to call the shots in our own lives.

The year before I joined the speed club I was having a minor religious crisis, the inevitable result of my mom's French Huguenot genes maturing to rational adulthood in a brain being bombarded by the teachings of Dad's Baptist church. Wichita's First Baptist was at that time a traumatized institution, recently divided by a Southern Baptist takeover attempt. Our church was part of the Northern Baptist Convention and had always been, but this was the era of Senator Joe McCarthy and his "red scares." Our pastor Reverend Thorne (his real name) had bought into prevailing accusations that the Northern Baptist leadership was honeycombed with communists, and he wanted us to switch conventions. My father was on the board of deacons that voted down the change. The Reverend, backed by most of our congregation, sued in court and lost. Temporarily stymied but unbowed, Dr. Thorne and his anti-communist brigade of twenty-seven hundred vacated the premises and founded a new Baptist church safe from Moscow's influence on the other side of the Arkansas River. They left behind a paltry three hundred of us commie sympathizers in an enormous four-story building that occupied nearly a quarter of a city block. The whole thing saddened my parents but I wasn't invested enough in the church to care. After the great divide I loved walking around on the upper, unoccupied floors of our place of worship where the silent halls felt full of ghosts.

It was Sunday school that brought on my crisis. There were the recitations, and the quizzes, and the direct questions from our teacher—all bear traps for me because through lack of interest I'd never learned my basic Shadrachs, Meshachs and Abednegos. When I was called upon, smiles cracked the faces of my more studious classmates as Mr. Smarty-Pants-Who-Thinks-He's-Too-Good-For-Sunday-School prepared to make an ass of himself again.

It wasn't that the Bible didn't interest me. It interested me a lot, but only in places. I found it interesting that King David couldn't keep it in his pants. Mary Magdalene and Delilah interested me so much I wanted to find out more about them than the Bible contains. Slayings in the Bible fascinated me because murder by rock is so gruesome, giving me a lot to imagine. God's cruelty to some of his most devoted and obedient followers, men like Job and Abraham, dismayed and mystified me.

Jesus interested me most of all. Him I loved. My attachment began in my preschool years when I learned he'd said, "Let the little children come unto me." A big framed reproduction of him hung on the wall of my Sunday school classroom and his soulful eyes looking down into mine were the kindest, most caring I'd ever known. They were even more loving than my mother's eyes. That portrait made me want to go to him, like he said—so he could talk to me and maybe hold me. Later I began to appreciate the importance of Jesus' main message to us: "Do unto others as you would have them do unto you." I saw it as the key to people getting along with each other, worded in the clearest, simplest terms so everyone could understand. I thought Jesus must be the wisest person who ever lived.

It was Sunday school I needed to escape. I talked it over with my brother, always one to game the system when possible, and we came up with a plan. Upon arriving at church the following Sunday we parted from our parents in the usual way and walked up the staircase that led to our Sunday school classrooms. But instead of getting off on the second floor where those rooms were located, we climbed to the unoccupied fourth floor and used its hallways to circle to the back of the building. There we descended stairs far from where our parents were entering Bible class for their indoctrinations and exited to the alley.

Our first mission began well. But soon a cold rain began falling on us and we found ourselves trapped in a diner a block up the street from our church. After we finished our cinnamon rolls, the manager, who could see by our Sunday suits we were pulling something on somebody, eyed us with disapproval as though he needed our booth to seat the nonexistent waiting customers in his all-but-empty establishment. We stayed where we were until the rain stopped, then walked back to the church and waited inside its Second Street entrance where we usually met our parents.

The next Sunday was windy and cold, but not too cold, so after our cinnamon rolls John and I walked around downtown to see what was happening. Mostly the autumn wind of the Great Plains was happening, dragging fast food sacks down empty streets and skipping paper cups. The only place we found open, other than another café, was Rector's Bookstore, a good place to warm our ears. We entered and were greeted by the sweet acidic smell of new paperback books. After browsing twenty minutes we hustled back to the church in time to pose as obedient children.

The Sunday after that we skipped the cinnamon rolls and went directly to Rector's and browsed. It seemed we'd developed a yen for poking around in paperbacks, though not yet for reading them. I was, at that time, an aficionado of cover blurbs, steamy passages, and the bewitching smell of printer's ink. Yet I perused many of the novels and story collections I would later buy and read. Probably I was sticking my toe in the water. During our explorations in that great old bookstore, gone now I believe, John and I left grubby boys' fingerprints on dozens of items yet never bought a single one, and the clerks never objected. Being in the trade, they knew how young innocents get hooked on their disillusioning products. I have to wonder, was Rector's open on God's day among all those churches to snare believers in crisis and spiritual drifters?

My brother and I became so comfortable in Rector's that, one Sunday, we lost track of time. On our return to the church we hurried around the corner onto Second Street and saw our parents standing outside on the sidewalk. They'd exited to look for their tardy sons and now they'd found us. With no other choices available, we walked to them. I did not like the look on Father's face. He almost never lost his temper but I could see he might. Mother was sad and disappointed and, knowing her, only some of the disappointment was in her sons. She would typically blame herself more than us for our failures, thinking she must have at some point incorrectly implemented the advice of America's pediatrician, Dr. Benjamin Spock. My mom was an alien in our land of shirkers and complainers, always looking for the way she was responsible—or at fault—for everything.

"Where have you boys been?" Dad asked.

I hated lying, to my folks or anyone else, so I told the truth.

"How long has this been going on?"

"Six weeks or so."

He looked at John. "Same for you?"

"Yes," said my brother.

"For now, let's go inside to the service. Your mother and I need to talk about this."

I don't remember our punishment. Likely we got grounded and took a hard swat or two on the butt with the ping pong paddle that lived on top of the refrigerator, ready at hand. My brother and I returned to Sunday school and the matter appeared settled.

Then one Sabbath morning two missionaries visited my class, a man and a woman just returned from a tour of duty in the Holy Land. They looked strong and tested, as persons might after extensive spiritual struggle in the desert. The woman did most of the talking. She informed us that in the Middle East and in Africa lived a vast horde of unfortunates cursed by their worship of a heathen god and destined for Hell. How could we who had seen the light let that happen?! She was hammering directly on my most fundamental objection to the cramped version of Christianity I was being fed. I couldn't understand a God so small-minded and so selfish he'd condemn most of humanity to Hell just for not worshiping him. I wanted to believe such a God didn't exist, but couldn't quite because I wasn't entirely sure.

The lady missionary riled me further by referring to the unfortunates as "Muslims" rather than "Moslems," the correct term, I was certain. Muslim was a *fabric*, wasn't it? I kept my rage bottled up in class and throughout the church service that followed and until I was riding home with the family. Then one of my parents gave me an opening and I let fly, berating the dolt who'd invaded our class with her narrow-minded views and mispronunciations. I wove my sarcastic attack with the skill that had convinced my folks I'd make a good attorney someday then added a dramatic capper: "I can't worship a God that sends dying babies to Hell for not believing in him!"

Some fathers would have stopped the car, pulled the first son from the backseat and delivered a physical wake-up call. My father turned to my mother and said, "Maybe, from now on, we should let the boys decide whether they want to go to church. What do you think?"

"I think that might be a good idea."

Dad caught my brother's eyes in the rearview. "John, next Sunday you and Bill can come with us to church or you can stay at home. It's up to you."

And that was it. My brother and I, together in the backseat, exchanged a look of disbelief. We hadn't dreamed our folks could be *that* accommodating. But sure enough, the following Sunday they went to church without us. As a condition of our release we were confined to the house until they got back. I was put in charge, and Mom left a list of phone numbers in the event of various emergencies. Then they were gone.

Freedom!

Wasn't it great!

The house seemed awfully quiet as I drifted down to the rec room where my brother had turned on the TV and was running through channels in the ancient mode—by turning a knob on the front of the set. We decided on a half-hour drama produced by the Catholic Church. It was followed by a similar show funded by the American Council of Churches. That morning we learned there were a bunch of these programs, all with a moral message and all seemingly aimed at misguided persons sitting at home feeling guilty while everyone else was in church.

Freedom was beginning to feel less wonderful than I'd anticipated. A malaise settled over me on that day and on subsequent eye-glazing Sundays until I discovered an antidote. One Sabbath morning, just to take my mind off the emptiness that was my life, I picked up something printed and began to read. I think it was a *Reader's Digest* but it may have been the newspaper or *Time*. Whatever the publication, my new relationship with it represented the sprouting of a seed perhaps planted weeks earlier in Rector's. Soon I was voluntarily reading books, transforming my Sunday mornings from wallows in boredom to golden hours of deliverance, when I traveled the earth on magic carpets woven from paper pulp. And there was a bonus. While enjoying myself I was developing my least-developed academic skill and one that would be essential to my adult life. Was Jesus behind it? Maybe it had been Jesus all along. Jesus who loved me and who therefore led me from the house of his Father into the Promised Land.

FIVE

ETWEEN the Alaskan concessions area and the skating floor stood a cinderblock wall with a wide passage at one end. Next to the passage was a window with large panes which had been painted over with lime-green paint. Several consecutive panes in the window had been removed from their muntins, creating an opening through which spectators could view the skating floor from concessions. When a night session was ending and our parents arrived to pick John and me up, they stood behind this opening and watched us skate. If I was tooling down the floor talking to somebody, I'd notice them, in their winter coats let's say, Dad wearing his gray businessman's fedora, Mom a colorful scarf. As my eyes met theirs they'd smile and wave. Both parents had smiles that radiated good will—open, generous smiles, my father's somehow enhanced by his crowded teeth, Mother's brighter for her small mouth. The picture I have of them waiting there patiently has become a symbol of my childhood security because they never missed, were never late, in fact always came early so they could see us skate and know who our friends were.

Quite a few speed club members liked talking to my folks, who spoke to young people the same way they spoke to adults, respecting each person's particular intelligence. During the years John and I skated, our parents made a number of skater friends, just as they made friends among rink parents, most of whom were a generation younger than them. It sometimes surprised me how much Mom and Dad were respected by almost everyone. Back then I thought it was because of their financial success, neglecting to consider that several rink parents were far better off moneywise and not as popular. Today I believe it was my parents' genuine interest in others that drew people to them. Skaters saw in them I think the outlines of the idealized fictional parents who visited us in our living rooms via television—couples like the Cleavers and the Andersons, mature, understanding, unshakably stable. Some of my rink friends probably would have traded parents with me gladly. And who could blame them? My brother and I knew we got a lucky draw.

On the night Katy and I became a couple, Mom and Dad surely watched us share the last couples skate. They would have known who Katy was because everyone at the rink knew who she was. I wonder now what they thought of us. They would have seen we looked good together—both well-constructed and proud. Probably they understood I'd found my first real girlfriend. Someday he's going to marry a girl like that they may have thought. And if that's what they thought, being who they were they would have wondered about Katy's family background.

SIX

 Y new girlfriend and I tried to attend sessions at the
Alaskan on the same nights, and we usually connected,
sharing every couples skate. I liked that and I think she
expected it. At first we were tentative with each other, to put it
mildly. Our three-minute tours through the whirling stars always
ended with us thanking each other politely then skating off in
different directions. As we spent time together though our anx-
iety levels fell and we began staying on the floor after the lights
came up. We circled and talked, though the talking was sporadic.
One of us would ask a question and the other would answer, then
a long silence as we scoured our brains for the next question.
Neither of us was much of a talker and we were in a precarious
predicament—in love for the first time and totally clueless, vir-
gins in every sense of the concept.

We learned the basics about each other. We'd both be in ninth
grade when school began, though Katy wouldn't turn fourteen
like me until early December. We attended different junior highs
but knew that in a year we'd be funneled together into East
High's enormous sophomore herd. We already knew each other's
grades. One afternoon weeks before we became a couple we were
standing in the bleachers waiting for a team photograph when

Katy, two or three rows behind me, called out my name. I turned
and looked up at her and she asked, "What are your grades?" Her
curiosity about that surprised me. I wasn't eager to come out as
a nerd to most of my teammates all at once, but I respected Katy
too much not to do it. "Straight As," I told everyone.

After we were a couple and I'd learned she *liked* me being a
nerd, I wondered whether my answer helped persuade her to
pick me for a boyfriend. It was good she admired my success in
school because it helped balance our relationship. I admired her
success in a sport we both loved. As to Katy's grades—"mostly
Bs"—that was fine with me. She was plenty smart, quick on the
uptake and sensitive to a fault, so her grades seemed unimport-
ant. I assumed she wasn't very interested in school. Later, after
I'd seen the distractions in her family life, I wondered how she
made Bs.

Some of the things I learned about Katy's family I learned
not from her but from friends at the rink and my brother. These
were things my girlfriend knew I'd find out but that she didn't
want to discuss with me. The main item was her parents' divorce
some years earlier. Divorce was fairly rare in Kansas in the 1950s.
Many people rather unkindly looked down on divorced parents
and sometimes their children. Charlotte Linsey was not only
divorced but lived with her boyfriend, compounding her sin.
People spoke lightly of her, and although I understood why, I
liked her because she was always sweet to me. Katy made every
effort to keep her mother and me apart and when she couldn't
she was on pins and needles every single second.

There was also Gloria's boyfriend Luke. I can't remember who
told me that his reason for being absent from the rink was a
ninety-day sabbatical at the P-Farm, Wichita's agricultural jail
facility for minor violators. Laid off from work and broke, he'd
used a stolen Coke machine passkey to loot a string of outdoor
vending machines in the middle of the night. During his crime

wave a cop on patrol pulled him over for a burned-out taillight, and when the officer decided to search the car he found the illegal passkey and Luke's collection of suspiciously undistinguished coins.

Luke's mistake wasn't exactly brilliant but I thought it showed guts. It was his relationship with Gloria that bothered me at first because she was so much younger. He was twenty-one, I believe, six years her senior. My attitude softened though as I got to know him. He was no cunning manipulator, rather the opposite—an impulsive guy with a big heart inclined to do the right thing. And Gloria was no teenybopper. Her role as stand-in mother was a serious commitment requiring adult behavior nearly all the time. I don't recall her ever losing control or even acting like a teen. She was so into her role I think she may have mothered Luke a little, though I never witnessed that. What I did see was him taking the father role in the makeshift family they'd created out of necessity and affection. He provided rides, a sympathetic ear, and protective muscle.

Gloria and her guy were probably the best attuned, smoothest functioning couple at the Alaskan and I think it was because they agreed completely on what was important. Both wanted a mate capable of giving and receiving unqualified love, something they found abundantly in each other. Gloria had gone outside her unstable family for her rock, while Luke was a guy who hadn't gotten many breaks in life and was trying to make the most of what he had—his slot on our Men's Relay, his black and gold muscle car, and his relationship with Gloria. He and Gloria were our club's most devoted members, maybe because rink society gave their love a place to thrive.

I always thought Gloria was quite pretty, as did everyone else, but I came to prefer her sister's more subtle looks, maybe because I loved her. When I think of Katy at thirteen or fourteen I remember her intense and guileless eyes so transparent

I was sure I could read her feelings even when she didn't want me to. Since everything happening inside her stayed inside, it was good I could read her, just as it was good she could read me. I'm sure we said more to each other by exchanging looks than we did with words. She was a small girl. Small body, small facial features, small even teeth like her siblings and mother, and little freckles across her nose and cheeks. She wore what most girls wore to the rink back then—a cotton blouse with its three-quarter sleeves rolled up above the elbow and its tail out and hanging over Bermuda shorts in the warm months and pedal pushers in winter. Both combos bugged me because they made vague the middle of a girl's figure, robbing beauty of its due I thought. The first time I saw Katy's slim lines in a swimsuit I had to look twice to believe my luck.

When racing, Katy gave it everything she had start to finish, like me. The distances we skated in our junior divisions were sprints and there was really no reason to hold back—though many skaters seemed to, pacing themselves perhaps, or perhaps trying to avoid falls. My longest race was the half mile, or 880, which made about the same demands on my lungs and muscles as a 220 in track, definitely a sprint. I can see Katy racing. She is coming out of a turn, leaning over the pylon, driving her legs and swinging her arms. Her fists are clenched, teeth gritted, every fiber in her tough little bod maxing out. Once I saw her round a pylon in the lead to find two skaters sprawled on the floor in her path. Without breaking speed and as adroitly as a ballerina she stepped over one girl and swerved around the other.

My girlfriend and I were alike in other ways. Sometimes it showed in small things. We both insisted on smelling good but overdid it by a factor of ten or more, me with Mennen's After Shave, Katy with a potent and alluring cologne appropriately named Ambush. We smelled so good that had someone struck a match too close to us we might have gone up in a fireball. Other

similarities were more important. We were both romantics, full
of high hopes for our love. We both believed in loyalty and valued courage over intelligence. Inwardly we were emotional, out-
wardly restrained. We were both strong willed. Unfortunately we
were also vain, a similarity that surfaced during our first summer
together.

I was getting most of my exercise at the rink rather than outdoors as in previous summers and looked pale in the mirror, a
ghost of my usual summer self. Deciding I needed more color,
I laid out one morning on our flat garage roof with a gym mat
under me, a book in hand, and an electric fan on an extension
cord not so much cooling me as blowing off sweat. No suntan
lotion of course because that would have defeated the purpose. I
wanted a *deep* tan. My only mistake was in measuring sun dos-
age. I baked until I was turning pink, which sane people know is
far too long. My burn gathered steam throughout the day until
by evening most of me was fire engine red, a shade as deep as I'd
hoped for but too intense. At the rink my achievement earned
me many congratulatory slaps on the back and some unkind
wisecracks involving lobsters and the like. Brother John, seeing
a way to kick me while I was down, divulged to everyone I'd
torched myself not while swimming or fishing but while sun-
bathing under a fan like some Hollywood starlet.

Around that same time, maybe to keep up with me, Katy tried
her own shortcut to a golden brown by applying liquid tanning
agent from a bottle to her face, neck, upper chest, arms, legs, and
well, I'm not exactly sure where else. The commercial product
worked as advertised in places and according to the manufac-
turer's warning in other places, producing an arresting paisley
effect. My girlfriend looked so unsightly that she hid out in her
bedroom for a week while her little brother announced updates
at the rink. When she finally reappeared, her chastened blue
eyes staring from a brown and beige mask, she called to mind a

poorly executed avant-garde painting. I started to comment but she stopped me. "I know," she said.

For all our similarities, there was one big difference. Our mothers. I began to appreciate this on a hot September afternoon when Charlotte Linsey drove Katy, our little brothers and me somewhere I can't remember. Mrs. Linsey was a short, plump woman who that day was wearing a white off-the-shoulders shift that revealed her undramatic but interesting cleavage. You could see her children in her face, though her face was rounder than theirs. She was in a great mood— laughing too much I thought— and I wondered if she'd been drinking. I would learn this was her sober self too.

All four car windows were down and the air blowing in was ovenlike, yet cooler than we were. Our brothers were in the front seat while Katy and I were in the back seat hugging the windows. Katy's mother was looking at us in the rearview and I thought she was worried about what we were up to. She quickly disabused me of that silly notion. "Katy, don't sit so far from Bill. He's going to think you don't like him."

"No he's not."

"Why are you lovebirds avoiding each other? If you sat closer you could hold hands." Silence as Katy stayed where she was.

Then a new tack. "Bill, why don't you move over next to her?"

"She's trying to stay cool, Mrs. Linsey. We both are."

"Bill, please call me Charlotte! Why do I have to keep asking you?"

Suddenly the radio was on at full volume. "HUTCHINSON NINETY-EIGHT! SALINA ONE-OH-ONE! TOPEKA NINETY-SIX!—"

"*Gregory!* Turn that off. We already know it's hot."

The radio went dead and snickers arose in the front seat. My brother and Greg were bonding. No surprise there. They reveled in the same cynical and scatological outlook.

Mrs. Linsey looked at me over her shoulder. "Please?" The car was drifting right.

"*MOM!*" Katy cried, "Watch out where you're *GOING!*"

The car jerked back on line, throwing me off balance and knocking Katy's head on the wing window.

"Bill?"

"Okay, Charlotte," I said. I would do it just to please Charlotte, and not only because Charlotte was nice to me. Charlotte wanted what I wanted, progress in her daughter's physical relationship with me. Charlotte seemed to think Katy was dragging her feet in the most consequential stage of female development and saw me as an ally in her campaign to get her kid moving. Although I felt guilty about this unspoken conspiracy, I never resisted it because I was young and male and when Katy was around, my mind was usually exactly where her mother wanted it.

SEVEN

T HE first time Katy visited our house her mother drove her. It was a Saturday afternoon a few weeks into ninth grade. Charlotte parked in the driveway and I let them in through the rec room door. My parents came down from the living room to say hi and to arrange a time for Katy's pickup, then Charlotte was gone, leaving behind an enticing scent and buoyant laughter echoing in our ears. My parents returned to whatever they'd been doing at the other end of the house and Katy and I found ourselves alone together for the first time.

I offered her a seat on the couch, puzzled by her look of dismay. To cover my confusion I stepped into my role as American host, asking if she wanted to watch TV. "Okay," she said, so I snapped on the set. The most entertaining show I could find among the three or four available back then was a fishing travelogue I sometimes watched. Its enthusiastic, fish-savvy host visited a new bass hotspot each week and filmed the damage he did to the local fish population. As casually as I could, I sat down next to Katy, who seemed to be wrapped up in the angling.

Over the next hour I osmosed myself close enough to my girlfriend that our hips touched and my arm lay behind her along the top of the couch. I was on tenterhooks and that's why my neck and shoulder muscles were cramping insistently as I made my next move—dropping my arm lightly onto her shoulders. She let it stay, her mouth grim as she stared at the TV. With my back muscles entering rigor mortis I knew I had to act. I leaned forward slowly to give Katy warning and aimed my mouth. Everything I'd seen on film and in photos and in life led me to expect her to close her eyes, part her lips, and tilt her head back, but instead she ducked my kiss—and I missed her! Her head popped up next to me, looking desperate. "I don't know *how*!" she announced, throwing up her hands.

Realizing she was even more afraid than me I tried to ease the pressure on both of us by admitting I'd never kissed anyone either, but thought we could probably figure it out by trusting to instinct. She must have liked that idea because she lost the look of a condemned facing the firing squad. Without further fuss she closed her eyes and turned her face up to me, holding still while I kissed her. It was far from a notable romantic achievement but that wasn't important. It was a rite of passage, and we met the ritual requirements well enough. In the process I found out Katy's lips were soft and that she smelled even better up close. Once we were hooked up I wasn't sure how long to wait before disengaging, so I killed time until I had to breathe again, then uncoupled. When Katy opened her eyes I saw relief. That's what I felt too. The deed was done. Our most difficult kiss was behind us, I hoped.

Later that afternoon I showed Katy around our house. Up in my bedroom, as autumn sunlight streamed in the windows, we stood with the dresser mirror reflecting our top halves and kissed again. This kiss was less self-conscious than the first, and I discovered that kissing Katy while our bodies touched was even better than doing it sitting down. I forgot to think about time and breathing and don't know how long we held it. I considered a third kiss but decided not to push our luck. We'd made a lot of progress for one day.

EIGHT

ATY and I grew up in the years following the most lethal military conflict in recorded history, helping explain why we came of age in an America whose leadership in all areas extolled the virtues of love, marriage and family to a population that overwhelmingly agreed. The golden trinity doesn't happen in a vacuum of course. It depends on people becoming couples first. And that's where institutions like the Alaskan Roller Rink came into play by providing appropriate places for people to meet and match up. I doubt roller rinks were designed specifically to promote population growth, but had they been, they couldn't have done a much better job.

At a typical rink in the late fifties, a couples skate was announced every half hour and all you had to do to participate was ask your heart's desire out on the floor to hold hands and roll with you for a few heart-thumping minutes. During this briefest and least demanding of dates you risked little, yet stood to gain much because magical things can happen even to level-headed people when bedazzled by flying starlight and immersed in wall-to-wall stereophonic mood music. Falling in love at the Alaskan was so easy that during the rink's four decades hundreds of couples must have done it—thousands maybe. I wasn't acquainted with all the romantic pairs who skated there even during my time, but I knew the couples on the speed club and some of the couples who were members of our affiliated group, the Alaskan Dance Club. Our more artistic cousins practiced their jumps and choreographies in the middle of the floor while we skate racers and everyone else revolved around them on the unmarked oval. Members of the two clubs represented the rink's inner circle, at least from our point of view.

Stan Preboth and his girlfriend Alice, both dance skaters, were one of the most prominent pairs at the rink. They were in their mid-twenties and their clout derived primarily from Stan's two necessary but seemingly contradictory roles. He was rink DJ *and* floor traffic cop. As DJ, he drew upon his unerring gift for picking the best from rock's top forty. He kept the sound cranked to a level we approved—loud but not quite loud enough to bring down the roof—and he announced the numbers and their artists with a fitting reverence. Although his teen years were behind him, he clearly shared our musical tastes. Rock's first golden era was then winding down and many rock fans were far from young.

After spinning the fast number that drove us guys like windup androids during Men Only, Stan would play a slower tune to calm us down as he switched hats to floor traffic patrol and began reinforcing the speed limit with authority. Any skater exceeding about ten miles an hour during a free skate received one or more piercing blasts from Stan's silver whistle. Stan would point at the violator and skewer him (usually a him) with a stern frown. In the unlikely event the violation continued, he would chase down the perp and tell him off. When our roller fuzz pursued a speeder he was amazingly swift despite his heavy dance skates. He cut no slack and would have busted his own grandmother for dropping a gum wrapper. We accepted his strictness because we realized it was necessary. Also Stan was extremely fair, with a large reserve of good will. If a skater needed somebody to talk to, our counselor on wheels was easy to find and ready to listen.

Physically Stan was a slight, handsome man of medium height with a mop of dark brown hair styled into a flawless pompadour that gleamed under the rink lights. His easy-going smile featured even teeth and a mild overbite. While on the job he wore the uniform of all rink employees, black slacks and a gold long-sleeve shirt with "Alaskan Roller Rink" embroidered in black cursive on the back. The uniform emphasized Stan's leanness, which may have been a result of his hyperactivity. It's hard to remember him without remembering him on the move. Rolling around the oval talking to somebody he'd suddenly whistle a violator into compliance, then as the record on the turntable ran out of grooves, he'd sweep across the floor through traffic and reach into his little green shack built into the rail and lift out the big silver mike. He'd introduce the next skate as its sound track began pouring from the speakers. Then back to law enforcement. He stopped moving only when Men Only or Ladies Only filled the floor with streaking bodies. Stan viewed these insanities from his shack like a lifeguard, making sure nobody got sucked under the thundering wheels.

Stan's girlfriend Alice had a pleasant, almost pretty face that appeared destined to never completely outgrow childhood. Her body was physically perfect in my estimation, magnetic beyond reason—with projecting breasts, a dancer's taut abdomen and hips, and incredibly shapely legs. When Alice and Stan were in shoes, observers with small minds might have thought her too much woman for such a mildly developed guy. But elevated on dance skates and moving to the music they were so artistically right no one could have questioned them. Totally attuned, they flowed with serene dignity, two bodies moved by a single mind, or so it seemed. Watching them you thought they had to be in love.

During some competition at the Alaskan several of us young male speed skaters were putting on our wheels in a dressing room when Alice walked in carrying a skate case and sat down on the bench opposite us. As she leaned forward to slip off her shoes and pull on athletic socks, her abundant white breasts threatened to spill out of her low-cut sequined top. It took her several minutes to lace the tall boots on her dance skates and I wasn't the only young naturalist following her every quiver as she cinched again and again and again. Her skirt was about as short as a skirt can be and still be a skirt (as opposed to a sash), and its brevity placed on public view her gorgeous legs from her boot tops all the way up to the holy grail, tastefully clad in white panties. In my days I've watched a big tornado sway by and I've watched Alice put on her skates and it's hard to say which natural wonder impressed me more.

My memory is that Stan and Alice didn't always have a smooth go of it in the non-skating part of their relationship. I think there was an engagement, later broken off, then another engagement. My take on them, based primarily on rumor, was that Stan wanted to settle down while Alice hadn't finished enjoying her life as a single. A girl with her looks can pretty much command her choice of partners and she might have been making up for lost time. Maybe she'd been shy in high school. Maybe she was just having fun.

After the recording "Mr. Blue" by The Fleetwoods was released late in 1959, Stan developed a strong attachment to this lament rendered in stirring harmonies by three high school friends, two girls with haunting voices and one lucky guy. Our DJ played the record really too often, maybe because he identified with the male vocalist whose love "paints the town" without him. Stan worked nearly every night, while Alice came to the rink only sometimes, so our Mr. Blue was often alone with the music, doing jumps in the center of the floor during couples skates while the romantic pairs circled him. I don't doubt Alice loved Stan. Sometimes when she looked at him you could see it. He was the kind of guy most of us expect to make a good husband and father, and I'm sure she valued that in him. I don't know whether they worked it out or not but I hope they did.

The oldest lover at the Alaskan was the grandfather of our reigning national champion in Juvenile A division, Ronnie Duncan. On Saturday nights Grandpa Duncan, in his sixties, brought his thirty-year-old girlfriend Ramona to the rink on a date. Grandpa had a balding pate, an erect fit body, and red suspenders. Grumpy he was not. In fact, he gave every indication of loving life to the hilt. Ramona was a plus-size brunette typically poured into a pair of loud pedal pushers, often flamingo or turquoise. Whether moving or sitting down she constantly tested every seam in her pants, most notably the one bisecting her lush mound of Venus.

Grandpa Duncan and his girl had their own style of couples skating and it was worth a view. They came down the floor side by side with their arms cross-hitched in front of them, weaving to the right then to the left as they sank and rose in a complex and skillful dipsy doodle that reminded me of a merry-go-round. I think their style derived from polka music Grandpa skated to in his early years because whatever was playing on the Alaskan's sound system he and Ramona moved to the polka beat. They sure seemed to make each other happy. Were they in love? Kind of looked that way. Back home at Grandpa's house there was a Grandma Duncan and I don't know her position on matters. She wasn't a skater, I guess, or had given it up.

NINE

LARRY Lucas was the Alaskan's Mr. Essential. During sessions he ran both the skate rental and the repair shop, all from one room. He maintained the rental skates and built custom skates for members of the speed and dance clubs. At the end of each session he closed the shop and became the rink janitor, manning a push broom as he chewed gum and scowled. First he swept the bleachers from the top down, then the skating floor from one end to the other, finally the concessions area and long hallway to the restrooms—pushing ahead of him a pile of dirt, cigarette butts, ticket stubs, dust bunnies, and oiled sawdust. Occasionally he took over behind the concessions counter for Clarence Hayes and his wife, the Alaskan owners. And when our DJ had to miss work with the flu, our essential one filled in for him.

In return for his thirty or forty hours of work each week Larry got enough money to support himself and, perhaps as important, a home of sorts. During his high-school years, arguments with his father had blown up so badly that Larry had walked out on his birth family and rented a small apartment. After the split I think the rink owners in some sense stood in as his guardians till he came of age. When I began skating Larry had just started to attend Wichita University. He planned to major in physics and since he was a bright, focused guy, I'd guess he followed through. He was quite good looking, with dark hair combed back on the sides, large brown wide-set eyes, and regular, chiseled features. He was built like James Dean and most of the time he projected a Dean-like nonchalance, a stance popular among older skaters and one Larry managed as well as anyone.

This was the wooly era when Westerns on television and in film spawned a fast-draw craze among America's dude cowboys. Larry succumbed to the fad, pulling for speed in his apartment until the day his .22 revolver ejaculated prematurely, spinning a slug into the back of his calf and out at the ankle. Fortunately, his through-and-through missed bones. A wound like that is nevertheless one for the emergency room, but I doubt Larry could afford it, and I'm sure he didn't want to be questioned by the cops, so he practiced a little frontier medicine. He poured a bottle of iodine down the long channel through his calf muscles then sealed the wound at either end with a plastic strip. The next day he was back on duty at the Alaskan, limping along behind his push broom with a more intense scowl. The rink small fry, who idolized Larry, saw him limping and of course had to hear the story of how he got wounded. When he complied, they wheedled for a peek underneath one of the strips until he finally gave in, acting disgusted.

Larry's most winning side emerged when he kidded around with his young admirers, as he did often. He would pretend to be an unreasonably angry man, blowing up over any minor slight, threatening to break bones. Every kid at the rink knew that all it took to get him going was an insult. He'd stop what he was doing and fix the offender with his snake eyes. "Leach, you little pecker. You just put your ass in a sling. You know that, don't you?" A big grin from Leach and gales of laughter from the peanut gallery. Larry would chase down and collar his detractor full of giggles, who after being tickled half to death and begging for mercy would be released.

Larry was a former national champion in the Intermediate Men Division and he'd won gold in Chicago on our A-team Men's Relay. His girlfriend Martina Eisley brought home two golds from Chicago for relay victories. Like Larry she was a college freshman and quite attractive. One difference between them was in residence. Larry occupied a bachelor pad in a declining neighborhood while his girlfriend shared her family's new four-bedroom ranch style in a toney east Wichita suburb.

Martina was a plush blonde with a soft, conventionally pretty face, full lips, and a fetching dimple in one cheek. She was physically alluring but her usual mood seemed a little downbeat to me. Not unhappy exactly. More like she didn't expect much out of life. Her relationship with Larry was stormy and full of frequent breakups and reconciliations. No more dramatic pair was then performing under the big top of the Alaskan, though Katy and I were about to give them a run for their money.

One warm evening in the early fall Martina and her folks threw a party at their house for the speed club. As night fell, rumbling hotrods tooled into the Eisleys' sedate neighborhood, shaking the social order with their barely legal mufflers. I don't recall who I caught a ride with but I do remember finding a fine party laid out for us. On the patio was a cooler of soft drinks, plenty of snacks, and a portable hi-fi stacked with forty-fives. Some of us were standing in the music talking when Larry burst out the back door and rushed through us. I wasn't able to get out of his way fast enough and he bumped my arm, sloshing cola out of my paper cup. He stormed through the yard gate and soon his heavily modified vehicle began shattering a peaceful night. His engine screamed as he laid rubber through first gear, making a terrible squall.

"What's with him?" I asked Charley Stover, the older guy I was talking to. Charley was a good friend of Larry's.

"He and Martina are fighting."

"What about?"

Charley wrapped a big hand around the back of his muscular neck and his brow furrowed. "Well, they're supposed to be in love but she's got hot skivvies." I searched his face to see if he was putting me on and realized he was embarrassed.

Maybe a year later a former speed club member who'd quit skating and gone on to other things revisited the Alaskan. Richard was overdressed for the rink in his new corduroys, expensive shirt and spotless beige trench coat. On his face was the smugness of someone who is slumming. As he and I talked in the aisle below the bleachers Martina appeared carrying her skates. She paused to scan the skating floor, looking for someone, and Richard with a knowing smile leaned close enough that I smelled his breath mint. "Looks like an angel, doesn't she? Well, she's not. I took her out one night and laid her in my back seat."

Since I'd already heard something similar from a more trusted source, I thought Richard was probably telling the truth. Beyond that I wasn't sure what to think. The situation seemed unfair to Larry, who so far as I knew didn't have hot skivvies of his own. Yet I had to sympathize with Martina because I shared her weakness, knowing personally the burden of hot skivvies. The very idea of Martina's hot skivvies in fact gave me hot skivvies, and I figured if I got the chance I might do what Richard did. But one thing I wouldn't do, I felt certain, was brag about it afterward. When a girl shares with you in that way, the least you owe her is gratitude and silence. I lost respect for Richard that night.

TEN

As I was becoming a competitive racer, another Junior Man on our team began joining me during free skates to talk. Rick Shafer and I learned we were both ninth graders at Roosevelt and, rather amazingly, had been born in the same hospital on the same night. Both of us were more girl crazy than most guys our age and we shared a taste for sarcasm too. Soon Rick began inviting me over to his house to use his weight room. I resisted at first because I wasn't sure I wanted him for a friend. He could be embarrassingly goofy, sometimes acting like a kid years younger.

He kept inviting me though until finally I went, lured by his weights. My own 110-pound barbell set was fine for doing reps (and for tripping over in the dark as I walked to and from my bed) but it was no longer enough iron to test my high end. Rick had stockpiled several hundred pounds of plates, more than I would ever need—and he was begging me to use them. I rode my bike over to his house and was introduced to his gym, which occupied one side of his family's two-car garage. He had lifting mats, a couple of weight bars, a big rack of cast-iron plates, dumbbells, a bench, a chinning bar, and a fan. "How much do you want to start with?" he asked.

He was loading plates on a bar when the door from the kitchen opened and his sister started down the stairs into the garage. Rachel, a year younger than us, was a female version of Rick—just as thin, just as good looking, and just as deeply tanned as he was. They shared the same bright brown eyes as well, though I remember Rachel's being brighter.

Rick glared at her. "Scram, creep! You're not wanted here!" The level of anger in his voice surprised me.

"It's my garage too. I can be here."

Rick dropped the weight wrench and bounded across the room and up the stairs. He grabbed his sister by the waist, turned her around and pushed her up the stairway toward the kitchen door while she resisted by bracing her feet against the risers. Rick was strong enough to force her to the landing but there she pressed the soles of her court shoes against the closed door and held firm. Her brother couldn't budge her. "Move it!" he barked. She didn't. Maybe she couldn't. He released one of her arms and slugged her hard on the thigh.

"Ow, that hurts!"

"It's supposed to hurt. Did you know you're missing Howdy Doody?"

"Let go of me!" Her feet were on the ground again and Rick's hands were clamped around her forearm, twisting in opposite directions with a vengeance. "Quit it!" she screamed.

"Then get out of here."

"You are so *mean*! You don't deserve a friend."

He released her arm and she entered the house. She didn't close the door all the way though and when Rick noticed he shot back up the stairs and slammed it shut. Then he returned to where I was. "Sorry you had to see that," he said.

I did several lifts with increasing weight. On the last one I wobbled and strained and emitted some pinched air, then pressed a new personal high. Afterward Rick and I did reps together, showing each other our programs. Then I decided to take off.

"Aren't you going to swim? I thought you came to swim."

"I didn't bring my suit."

"Use one of mine."

"Maybe next week."

"Have a coke before you go."

We leaned against the kitchen counter sipping our drinks and talking until something took Rick away, leaving me alone in the kitchen. A framed photograph on the wall caught my eye and I walked over and examined it. It was a black and white of high quality taken probably in the 1940s. In it two men and a woman stand next to a light prop plane in a desert. Low, treeless mountains are in the background. One of the men is wearing leather headgear and a flight jacket, identifying him as the plane's pilot. The other man is dressed as though for safari, in khaki slacks and a khaki shirt. His thin build and narrow nose made me think of Rick and I assumed it was his father, whom I hadn't yet met.

Rick's pop looks very happy. His smile, the exotic locale, and the exotic lady beside him all proclaim "honeymoon." The bride is much younger than him, with long, straight, obsidian hair and the Asiatic features of a Native American. Her belted slacks and well-cut sleeveless blouse suit her thin frame. Her face in the photo is barely the size of a dime, yet her beauty is unmistakable. I never learned how this Indian princess met and married her aircraft company executive, so for me that photograph became the myth of their union, revealing nothing for certain but suggesting a lot.

Later that summer I pedaled over to Rick's house again, this time with my swim trunks. I changed into my suit in my friend's basement bedroom and when I came out he asked if I'd like to meet his mom. I followed him down a hallway to a closed door where he knocked, then entered. We passed through a beaded curtain into a dimly lit room filled with the voice of Frank Sinatra crooning to his band. I remember wondering how anyone, even an adult, could be hooked on such sleepy music in the age of Little Richard and Jerry Lee Lewis.

Rick's mother was reclined in an easy chair and surrounded by a subtle fragrance. She held a large plastic glass of what looked like iced orange juice on the arm of her chair. I could see in her the girl in the framed photo—but twenty years older and with a woman's curves. Her once-long hair had been cut short and attractively feathered in a style that went well with her prominent cheekbones. She had on a loose housedress and her evening makeup matched the mood of the music. All in all, she looked a little too good to be a friend's mother. Under the perfume I detected alcohol, calling to mind the rumors I'd heard about Mrs. Shafer sometimes hitting the club scene in search of a good time. As her confident brown eyes rested on me I saw she still had what the younger woman in the photo had—the assurance that when she faced off with most men she held the aces.

"Mom, this is Bill. I told you about him."

"Hello, Bill," she said in a smoky voice.

"Hello Mrs. Shafer."

As I stood next to her chair with my rolled towel under my arm, her hand slipped into mine. Her palm was soft and cool and thrilling. She smiled up at me. "So you're going with Katy, huh?"

I was always glad to acknowledge that.

"You two make a good couple."

"Thank you."

"You must be a fast skater."

By asking a series of flattering questions she got me talking about roller skating, people at the rink, my parents, my classes at school, cafeteria food at Roosevelt, and so on. Finally she ran out of questions, though she continued holding my hand. I looked at my friend to see what he thought. He seemed pleased that his mom and I were hitting it off.

Her parting words were, "Come see us again, Bill. You're welcome here."

Rick told me later that both his parents were in favor of our friendship on account of my grades. They thought I'd be a good influence on him. Actually, I influenced his grades only when I did his math homework for him. His influence on *my* grades however was probably large, and that's because our developing friendship helped me deviate from the straight and narrow path my parents had guided me onto with such care. Rick was a rule breaker by nature and by calculation, and this was attractive to me because I found myself in the position of an actor who's become typecast in a boring role. All my life I'd been the good student and good boy most parents want, but my goodness had begun to smother me. I'd decided there must be more to life than pleasing my parents and being good. Friendship with Rick promised to give me a taste of the wild side.

Rick and I were taking turns on the diving board when his sister walked toward us across the lawn in a one-piece suit. Rick scrambled out of the pool and went for her. She turned her back against his onslaught, then resisted as he pushed her toward the house.

"Stop it!" she yelled. "It's my pool too."

The scene in the garage a month earlier repeated, ending as it had then, with Rachel being driven back into the house. I felt uncomfortable swimming while she couldn't, so I hung out just long enough to be polite before shoving off. Although I found my friend's behavior impossible to defend, I could see that Rachel was something of an instigator. She looked for opportunities to make her brother look bad in front of me. Since I liked them both, I stayed out of their squabbles.

Later I got to know one of Rick's close buddies at the rink,

Kyle Diller, who gave me deeper insight into Rick. Kyle was tall, square shouldered and overweight, with long dark hair he oiled, parted and combed back on both sides of the part. He was a regular at the Alaskan and was on the speed club for a time. I liked him but noticed that bad things seemed to happen to him. A ten-inch scar wrapped halfway around of one of his beefy forearms. It was an inch wide in the middle, snow white, and scary. As Kyle told it, he'd been walking home through Wichita University parking after a night basketball game when he was jumped by several neighborhood kids. During the scuffle one of the boys laid him open with a straight razor. Kyle swore he'd done nothing to provoke the attack, and at the time I took him at his word.

Months later, on a hot, sticky summer night at the Alaskan, rear door guard Ted Irving had opened the fire exit and set up one of the rink's huge commercial exhaust fans on the concrete apron just outside the building. When I skated by I saw Ted seated in his folding chair in the wash from the fan while talking to Rick and Kyle. I rolled through the tunnel and joined them on the apron, realizing they'd found the coolest spot at the rink.

The four of us were bullshitting around when I must have said something Kyle took wrong. I didn't know I'd offended him until he stepped in front of me and snapped a stiff jab into the middle of my face. He knocked me off balance and I reeled on my skates, trying to stay upright. He hit me again, this time above my ear. Then again. On wheels I was helpless, unable to throw an effective punch while Kyle, in loafers, used his stability and superior weight to happily pound my head. I realized he was going to take me apart if I didn't do something.

As he closed with me to jab again, I planted my toe stops on the apron and lunged, wrapping my arms around his neck. I bent my knees, pulling him forward and off balance and took him with me to the concrete. Once he was down his weight became a problem for him. He was struggling to get up when I pushed him on his back and climbed aboard. Pinned mostly by his own mass, he watched as I straddled his stomach and began swinging into his face. He blocked most of the punches with his arms but enough got through to punish him. I beat on him till my anger leaked away, then asked if he was ready to quit.

"No fucking way! Fuck you, Hart!"

I hit him some more but I'd lost my enthusiasm for the project. Now I just wanted the fight to end. After another dozen punches I asked again if he'd had enough.

Through a bloody grin he said, "You punch like a pussy. Eat shit!"

His attitude worried me. When a guy doesn't mind you beating the crap out of him how do you make him surrender? I gave him a few more stiff shots to the head then told him I was going to let him up, but if he tried anything I swore I'd choke him out, take off his pants and throw them up a tree. I let him contemplate that indignity then stood up fast on my toe stops, ready to grab him if I needed to. He rose ponderously to his feet, turned his back on the three of us and walked away through the parking lot with his shirttail out and his long hair hanging down over his ears. Although he'd asked for it, I felt sorry for him.

Neither Rick nor Ted had lifted a finger to stop the fight—and I hadn't expected them to. Teenagers don't stop fights because fights are too interesting. Fights determine winners and losers. I'd won but I wasn't feeling like it. I'd just beaten up somebody I thought was my friend and I felt like crap. "What did I say to piss him off?" I asked the guys.

"Got nothing to do with you," Rick said.

"It doesn't?"

"Kyle's mad at his mom."

ELEVEN

RICK'S attitude toward the opposite sex differed from mine, at least on the surface. Instead of looking for one girl to hold, be held by, make love to if possible, and maybe eventually marry, he cast his net wide and repeatedly, dating prospects in sequence just to see where each relationship led. As soon as he determined that a particular candidate was not going to sign up for his full-sex program he moved along—that is if his partner hadn't beat him to it. His reputation had been slinking around the Alaskan among the teen girls for a couple of years, yet he could always find new chicks for his queue, probably because of his dark good looks and maybe also because of his devil-may-care panache. That could be appealing when he didn't overplay it. He was usually flush moneywise and that never hurts.

One weekend night when Rick and I were fourteen he slept over at my house. We were under the covers of my double bed talking about girls when he explained his grading scale for potential romantic partners. Rick's A was for Angels, barely been kissed. B for Behaved girls, kissers and little else. C for still Chaste girls, tested but intact. And D for the girls who'd Done once or twice what Fs did Frequently. Rick's grading scale helped him zero in on his most promising targets—the Ds and Fs. He ran through the names of half a dozen girls we both knew at the rink, giving each a grade. Some of his grades surprised me, others didn't. When he was done I wondered why he hadn't mentioned Katy. Curious, I asked about her grade.

"A plus!" he blurted. Then he started laughing. He laughed loud and long, making clear how funny Katy's grade was to him. It wasn't so funny to me. Was he suggesting my girlfriend was ice sculpture or something like that? I knew she wasn't. She was just inexperienced. When Rick realized I wasn't sharing his happy moment he canned his amusement and answered more seriously. "What I mean is, Katy *was* an A plus. But since she met you she's gone down to an A or an A minus, or maybe a B plus. Maybe even a B or a B minus." As my girlfriend's grade sank, I wondered how low I wanted it to go. Not too low. Katy's innocence was one of the things I liked about her. Being the first guy she ever kissed—and the only guy she'd ever kissed—made me feel lucky. I could see that Rick's grades weren't going to work for me because I didn't view girls his way. Unfortunately, his thinking left its mark. I never quite got over the uncomfortable feeling that my relationship with Katy might be something to snicker at. We were such young lovers and so gone on each other that many at the Alaskan must have seen us as the rink darlings, as puppies in love. Maybe we were puppies, but it didn't feel that way to us.

On a school night around this time Rick and his girl of the month double-dated with Katy and me for a trip to a bowling alley. We left from the rink and didn't tell our parents we were going. I was a little uncomfortable with that but saw the others weren't. Rick's date, Roberta Dunsmore, drove us all in her car. Roberta was sixteen, two years older than the rest of us and many years more mature. She had a rep at the Alaskan as a tough girl though she may not have been one. She did look tough, with high cheek bones, narrow eyes, and a small stoic mouth on a rather cute face marked by a few pimples. I have a mental picture of her standing like a lean cowboy in men's jeans and a speed club jacket, her hands jammed in its pockets. According to the rink rumor mill, Roberta was not only a tough girl but also a fast girl, which explained Rick's interest in her to my satisfaction.

The man behind the shoe rental counter spotted trouble the moment we trooped into his alley with Rick leading. Our irrepressible friend was stooped over, jaw slack, knuckles swinging for the floor in the manner of an entitled orangutan. The rental man's face clouded up and stayed that way as he supplied us begrudgingly with bowling shoes. Roberta, embarrassed, stood apart from her date, looking more stoic than usual.

Since Katy and I had never bowled before, we let our friends go first so they could show us how to do it. Roberta led off, appropriately enough, being our best role model. During her graceful delivery she laid the ball down on the wood so softly you barely heard it touch. It whispered over the boards and drove into the pins, mixing them up with a satisfying rumble. She may not have gotten a strike that first throw but during the course of her game she made several and converted most of her spares. She showed us how to do it as well as anyone could have. Bowling to me is a physical Rorschach test, revealing important aspects of the bowler's personality, and in Roberta's case every roll was a testament to her pride and her perfectionism.

Rick was a guy who couldn't resist performing for an audience. True to form, he seized the opportunity to flamboyantly disrespect every facet of this hallowed pastime handed down to us by our British forebears. For his opening act he placed his ball on the foul line then gently nudged it forward. I was amazed that a bowling ball traveling so slowly could continue on a straight line *and* maintain its negligible momentum. When it finally met the pins and pushed through them, a few toppled but most remained upright as they were almost politely shunted aside into clusters. The automatic pinsetter swept the deck then faithfully reproduced this grotesque spare as Rick filled the building with the high-pitched, loony yucking I was coming to know too well. His subsequent rolls were equally attention grabbing. He imitated a football center by hiking the ball through his legs. He kicked the ball off the foul line with his foot. He bowled backward, sideways and lying on his stomach. Meanwhile his date's face grew ever grimmer. I wondered if she'd brought us to her home bowling alley.

Katy gave her all, as usual, but she wasn't built like the founders of the sport, athletes as well-rounded as the kegs of mead they laid waste to. My girlfriend's low body weight made ball control not so easy and she tried to compensate with muscle power. Further complicating her delivery were her small fingers, which I think were the reason she held onto the ball too long. Put it all together to understand the sight we witnessed on her first "roll." The ball, swung with surprising force, rose higher than Katy's head and came down about ten yards up her lane with a resounding thud. Every face in the building turned our way. The ball streaked into a gutter and rattled in the groove before rolling away harmlessly. A warning came over the public address. "Please do not loft the ball!" The man behind the shoe counter, holding a mike to his face as he glowered at us, had with the authority in his voice just identified himself as the alley manager.

Katy's second throw was even more spectacular. Again the ball rose above her head but this time it came down hard in the lane to the left of ours where it soon found a gutter and scampered off. A more forceful warning boomed from the PA: "BOWLING OUTSIDE YOUR LANE IS STRICTLY PROHIBITED!" Katy, crestfallen, returned to the booth and scooted in next to me. I started to explain that she needed to let go of the ball sooner but she didn't want to hear it. She'd had enough bowling and refused to throw again. As I was learning, she was someone who wanted to be good at everything she did, and when she thought she couldn't be good at something, she bailed.

Based on what I'd seen Roberta do, and on what I'd seen the pro bowlers on television doing, I'd concluded that making a strike required throwing the ball hard enough to really scramble the pins. Following this theory I fired a cannonball directly at the one pin. My ball flew into the wedge on target and mixed the pins with a violence that looked and sounded right—but it apparently lacked something because two pins remained upright. The standing pins, as luck would have it, were as far apart as they could be. I was facing the highly undesirable seven-ten split, which I of course failed to convert.

Although I bowled for several years I never advanced my game much beyond this point. I watched my friend John Myer (who became a litigator) develop a hook that curved his ball into the one from the side, producing more strikes and fewer splits. I saw all the pros using similar hooks to score 250 and above. So it wasn't that I didn't know how to get better. It's that I liked rolling the ball straight as an arrow. I improved my game a little by striking the one off center, and I got good at converting spares, which is fun. But I never became a good bowler, though I once rolled a 203. Bowling revealed me to be someone who insists on doing things his own way even when he knows his way is not the best.

After our night at the lanes, Rick and Roberta as a couple were kaput.

TWELVE

THAT fall Katy and I began going steady and exchanged name bracelets, which we bought just to go steady. Each bracelet had a nameplate and an attractive chain that encircled the wrist. I liked wearing Katy's name on my arm because I was proud to be her boyfriend, but going steady seemed like something we were doing just because everybody did it. It was our love for each other that would keep us faithful, not going steady.

There's another piece of jewelry from back then I remember better—a small heart-shaped gold locket on a gold chain that I bought Katy for her fourteenth birthday. I was looking for her gift in Sears when I saw the locket in a jewelry case and knew immediately it was perfect. Its price surprised me, several times what I'd been planning to spend, but as I thought about that I realized the price was right. Both locket and chain were fourteen karat gold, and besides, the perfect gift shouldn't come cheap. To buy it, I cleaned out my savings and went into debt to my parents. Katy seemed pleased with the gift and I loved it on her. When she wore a low neckline, the locket hung small and elegant between her shapely collar bones and above the cleavage she at that time mostly aspired to. At the rink she dropped it down her blouse before racing in Ladies Only.

Around that time I visited Katy at her house in the suburbs of east Wichita. I was familiar with the exterior of her family's beige two-story contemporary frame from the times we'd picked her up there and dropped her off. On this day I was the one getting dropped off, finally able to see the interior of her home. I was impressed by its spaciousness and modern design. It made my own house, built four decades earlier, seem cramped and quaint. Everything in the Linsey's place was new and their foyer had a twenty-foot ceiling.

Katy's mother fixed us colas over ice in big plastic glasses. Then she led us into the living room and guided us into the same easy chair. I wasn't sure why she did that but I approved. Her daughter and I were slim hipped enough to sit side by side comfortably and it was nice being so close to Katy that our arms and legs touched. The cloud of Ambush engulfing me was already working its mojo. Charlotte asked if we wanted the TV on, and we did, so she got it going then left the room. I heard her ascend to the second floor. Her footsteps passed overhead and a door closed, followed by silence. Katy and I were alone and I assumed we would be for some time.

We began exchanging the gentle kisses that had become our style during the few opportunities we'd had to practice. Kissing while wedged in a chair is awkward though, and hard on the neck, so I said, "This might be easier if you sat on my lap." She liked the idea and arranged herself sidesaddle, resting her calves on the arm of the chair. That worked great.

With all the privacy we could have wanted, we began holding our kisses longer, and though they were tender kisses their effect was cumulative. Slowly we got carried away, losing track of time as we followed the promptings of our bodies. Only in fantasies had I done the things I was doing. Gradually unbuttoning Katy's blouse. Easing down the zipper on her Bermudas. Touching her inside her clothes. Comfortable in her own home, she was letting herself be drawn into something I doubt she would have permitted elsewhere.

At first I didn't understand what she was doing, probably because it didn't mesh with my conception of her. In movements so tiny I could barely feel them, Katy was rubbing her seat on the very spot that was most arousing for me. Maybe she thought I wouldn't notice or maybe she was so far gone she didn't realize what she was doing. Her subtle rocking fed my imagination, making me queasy with excitement. My girlfriend seemed to be on autopilot, abandoning her inhibitions as she fell deeper into a bottomless kiss. I switched off my brain and jumped in after her.

A scraping sound on the front porch pulled me out of my reverie seconds before the front door swung open and our little brothers burst in, throwing a flood of sunshine on the runaway romantic entanglement in the easy chair. Katy's panic and my own were met with snotty giggles. Mortified, Katy clutched her unbuttoned blouse with one hand and her unzipped Bermudas with the other and ran for her bedroom, slamming the door behind her. I let the little mood wreckers pass by me with knowing grins, then stood up with an erection cramped painfully in my jeans and limped to a nearby bathroom. I had to pee but was so aroused I couldn't deflate for several minutes.

A glance in the bathroom mirror gave me a shock. I barely recognized my own face, distorted by lust much as Randy Santeer's had been that day in seventh grade math. I did not want to be another Randy. My leering mask nauseated me. I wanted to disown it, yet how could I? Making out with Katy had been the most moving experience of my life. Desire was still warm in my gut and what I really wanted was to repeat everything we'd done and keep going until we found out where it led. I now assumed sex with Katy would happen someday because I'd learned that my chaste, high-minded girlfriend could with a little encouragement get just as worked up as me.

I had an uneasy awareness that part of my childhood had been left behind that afternoon. I felt destined for a place I knew almost nothing about. I wondered if I'd be as happy there as I'd been in the safe, familiar world of my boyhood. I knew I might not be happy there at all, but I was going there for sure because I'd fallen under the power of something I didn't want to fight.

THIRTEEN

Y brother and I were in school when Mother had her first coronary. I remember Dad talking to us in the living room that evening. He called the thing by its name, "heart attack," but soft-peddled the event, saying it wasn't serious and that Mom was "going to be just fine." All she needed was "a few days rest in the hospital." Well, she rested at least a week before the doctors decided she was well enough to receive a visit from her sons. I asked Dad if Katy could go.

We picked her up at her house and when she opened the front door to me I saw her dressed up for the first time. It was one of the nicest surprises of my youth. My quite pretty girlfriend had become a beauty. She was wearing a dress that was perfect for her, a white satin juniors number hemmed at the knee and cut low enough on top to show the gold locket resting against her healthy-looking upper chest. Her sun-bleached hair, freed from its ponytail, fell to her shoulders, giving her a more sophisticated, grown-up look. Pink lipstick and a touch of eye shadow enhanced that look. The dramatic change in her appearance reminded me of Cinderella and I wondered why Katy didn't wear her hair down all the time. Today I can understand. For someone with her practical mindset that probably would have required too much fussing. Yet she'd chosen to fuss on this day, maybe with her sister's help.

As we entered Mother's hospital room she smiled up at us from a pillow. It was her familiar smile—bright, slightly buck-toothed, and infectious. It meant in this case that she was fine, no damage done, despite her dispirited hospital hair, the drip feeding her wrist, and the monitoring machines calibrating her grip on life. As her smile faded I noticed she looked older, quite a bit older. She looked tired too. It hit me then, as it hadn't before, that she'd actually suffered a *heart attack*. People died of those! I tried imagining my world without my mom and drew a blank. Maybe I was afraid to imagine such a world.

"I'm glad you came, Katy," my mother said. "You look so pretty."

"Thank you, Mrs. Hart. I hope you get better soon."

"That's sweet of you, dear."

Watching them together I was struck by Katy's respect for my mom. I hadn't noticed it earlier though it must have been there. My girlfriend's humble body language and soft voice would have been appropriate in talking to a saint. Katy probably found in my mom the qualities she missed in her own mom, and while she couldn't become my mother's daughter, she could become her daughter-in-law. I think she wanted that at least as much as she wanted to be with me. She may have dressed up that day to make a good impression on the family she hoped to join.

Late in the visit I wondered if bringing Katy had been a mistake. I thought Mother might be uncomfortable sharing her room with such a striking tribute to feminine youth, loveliness and good health at a time when she herself lacked those qualities more than she ever had. Besides, the visit was supposed to be about our family supporting Mom, not about Katy and me spending time together. Katy's resemblance to an underage bride, purely a matter of chance, couldn't have helped matters. But if my mother felt in any way put upon, neither Katy nor anyone else was allowed to notice.

FOURTEEN

I think Katy expected me to treat her the same way Luke treated her sister. Luke lavished his time and attention on Gloria like a bridegroom on the honeymoon, understandable since he *was* her husband in all but legal terms. His attentive example was far beyond me, a novice in the art of love. I was at that stage of male maturation when the call of my fellow young apes was often more compelling than togetherness with Katy.

The Alaskan's simian tribe was large and ranged in age from eleven or so to about sixteen. Any baboon wearing snap jeans and no belt was asking to have his denims yanked down from behind by one of his tribal brethren. Any undefended chimp shoulder might receive, from out of the crowd, a streaking flesh-and-bone RPG. Wrestling matches pitting two or more gibbons would flare up at random and roll around on the skating floor or up in the bleachers until quelled by Stan Preboth's soul-piercing whistle.

One ape behavior I remember well was notable for its creativity and violence. It began circulating the rink during a Saturday matinee and kept finding new victims deep into the evening session as male speed club members one after another got sucked in. The perpetrator would set up his dupe with a challenge: "You're such a punk that two of my fingers are stronger than your whole arm." The dupe would deny that, then be invited to participate in a contest that required him to sit down, rest an elbow on his knee and make a fist. The con would hook the upright fist with two fingers and pull it slowly down and away from the mark while the mark resisted. Through the wonders of leverage two fingers will always win this contest. That night many proud arms, swelling with veins and shaking, descended toward defeat.

At that point the two fingers would be abruptly withdrawn from the contest, releasing the fist stoked with kinetic energy to fly into the face of the hapless pigeon. The more the pigeon had to prove, the harder he popped his own beak. One of Rick Shafer's buddies put a big knot in the middle of his over-tanned forehead. Fortunately nobody lost a tooth or broke his nose. Katy watched me devote myself to such monkeyshines while Luke sat in the bleachers with her sister, discussing bedroom curtains.

Eventually Katy's tolerance ran out, I guess, and she came up with a plan to awaken me to my courtship duties. She knew that several guys at the rink carried a torch for her. Most guys are cagey about such things, so I don't know how many there were, but I do know she never ran short of boys to flirt with. And when she flirted, my demure and sensitive steady threw herself into the role with the passion of a ham actress commanded by her director to pull out all the stops.

The first time I saw Katy play coquette was a memorable event, though I can't remember who the guy was. I had my eyes on Katy and could barely believe what I was seeing. I would never have imagined she could be so fickle—or so talkative for that matter! The well-mannered Katherine the Silent whom I loved, the girl who communicated with monosyllables and her eyes, had shifted shape into Chatty Kathy. She looked foolish to me, jabbering so hard her ponytail shook. I thought it might be something she'd picked up watching her mom in action.

One guy Katy flirted with was Larry Lucas, bullet-scarred hero of the younger skaters, a nineteen year old respected by everyone at the rink. Larry was the last person I wanted Katy flirting with and probably that's why she chose him. He was a wonderful partner for her performances. When I was around to notice they'd ham it up together, Larry grinning like a fool and rolling his eyes and in every way acting totally smitten. It was their togetherness that killed me. They were mocking me!

Actually, it was more complex than that. In the middle of flirting Katy would sometimes turn around and look my way to see how I was taking it, inadvertently revealing her true intentions. I'm sure this bugged Larry, who could see he was being used, and in his over-the-top scenes with my girlfriend I think he was mocking her along with me. I should have seen this at the time because it was kind of obvious but my jealousy got in the way. I worried that when Katy and this handsome older guy saw their chance they were going to sneak off to Larry's broom closet.

Another of Katy's dependable flirts was Danny Swafford, a more real threat because he was probably in love with Katy and much nearer her in age. He was one of the most talented racers on our club, a muscular teen with a roughly handsome face who seemed to regard me as an amusing temporary obstacle. Whenever he saw Katy and me at odds he'd look for his chance to pull her Chatty Kathy string, setting her off. She'd repeat the same routine she used with Larry, though with less devotion, Danny being a year behind her in school. If I was out on the floor, every time I came around the oval I'd see them standing together at the rail, Katy laying it on while Danny held my eyes and grinned triumphantly like the fellow ape he was. When Katy wasn't around, Danny and I were able to build a stable young male relationship based on our ability to absorb devastating punches to our shoulders without wimping. We became pals in that limited way, a shoulder thumping brotherhood of two.

Katy and our speed club coach flirted in such a charming way you almost couldn't call it flirting. It was an innocent, wholesome sort based on mutual respect. Coach Fite was a former Army sergeant with a deadpan face that projected a cigar when he wasn't talking, and he didn't talk much. He found Katy delightful and although he rarely cracked a smile for any reason, he would perk up when she was around. He called her by her last name and spoke to her with the same gruff tone he used with the guys he liked.

At men's speed club practice one Saturday afternoon Coach was on the floor in his dance skates timing each of us for a single lap. Katy, in her court shoes, approached in the aisle below the bleachers. She came to the rail and Coach looked up at her. "Your practice ended an hour ago, Linsey. Can't do much for you now."

"I wanted to tell you why I missed."

"I know why you missed."

"Why?"

"Last time it happened you said your watch stopped. You're probably going to tell me that one again."

"My watch *did* stop." She was smiling now. "I bumped it on something and it conked out."

"Likely story."

"Well, it's true. Today my mom was late getting around."

"And why am I hearing this?"

"I didn't want you to think I forgot."

"I promise not to think that."

It was easy to understand why Coach and Katy liked each other. He'd trained her and she'd made them both proud. They also had the military connection. Katy's dad was a Marine veteran of the South Pacific, Sergeant Fite an Army veteran of Korea. I enjoyed watching Coach and Katy kid around because it brought out a winning side in each of them I wouldn't have known about otherwise.

It was a different matter when Katy flirted with guys our age. That really got to me. I didn't flirt with other girls—so why was she flirting? I knew of course that I could get back at her by doing what she was doing, but I wasn't tempted because I would have had to fake an interest in girls I wasn't interested in. That I refused to do. I came up with a different way to retaliate, one that raised the stakes.

On a night when Chatty Kathy was rapping the ears off some admirer, I waited, killing time until a couples skate was announced and Katy left her beau of the moment (as I knew she would) and began skating my way. I skated toward her and when we met I took her hand. But instead of pushing off with her into the revolving pairs, I stopped, turned her palm up and dropped her name bracelet into it, saying "Why don't you go steady with [Mr. X]? You two make a great couple."

"You're breaking up with me?"

"Not at all. I don't want to stand in the way of your happiness so I'm bowing out."

She looked lost for a moment—then blew a fuse. She fumbled with my name bracelet and couldn't get it open. Disgusted, she pulled it off over her hand and threw it on the floor at my feet and skated away.

I'd expected to feel really good after putting Katy firmly in her place. Instead I felt hollow, my first clue that breaking up wasn't going to be as easy as I'd imagined. I walked home under the stars with a cold wind pushing on my back and dead leaves racing past me in the street. I raged at Katy for flirting, at myself for handing her off thoughtlessly to another guy, and at the stars for observing my agony with such detachment.

At home I tried watching TV with the parents but was too distracted to follow Jack Paar's monologue. I went to bed intending to sleep then tortured myself for hours with a loop tape of the disastrous evening. After twisting my sheet into a ball of knots, I wept. Finally I fell asleep, certain I'd lost Katy.

Dawn brought new hope, of course, as it often does. I began thinking Katy might *not* have thrown herself into someone else's arms. Maybe she still cared for me. What if I apologized for breaking up and admitted I'd gotten jealous? Would she listen? Would she recognize the part she played? Would she forgive me? At the rink, she did listen. She forgave me and swore the boy she'd been talking to was just a friend. It was me she loved. We traded name bracelets again and returned to being a couple. I was so glad to have her back I managed to meet her expectations for a time and life was good. But nothing had actually been resolved.

FIFTEEN

I N the late 1950s American space experts were confident the Russians were inferior to us in high tech, right up until the commies launched the first satellite into earth orbit. Before we could respond in kind, they boosted the first dog into orbit, thumbing their noses at *our* technological insufficiency. Taken aback but hardly defeated, our leadership searched for ways to catch up with and surpass our enemies. American education experts thought they had the answer, arguing that our weakness lay in our naive egalitarian practice of mixing eggheads with also-rans in high school classes, bogging down the brainpower with dunderheads. Their fix was tracking. Schools were encouraged to provide a hierarchy of classes in each core subject, dividing up students by standardized test scores to make sure eggheads rubbed craniums only with other eggs. In a few years the craze metastasized to school districts throughout the country and to many college campuses, contributing, I think, to social stratification more rigid than makes sense in a democracy.

As a test-certified nerd I found myself in honors classes from the time my junior high succumbed to the mystique in 1958 until I graduated college nine years later. Hindsight tells me I profited from the experience by receiving a sound fundamental education from bright and committed teachers. But, as I mentioned earlier, I disliked the scarcity of girls in my honors classes, and I disliked the way tracking separated me from many of my friends. The guys I walked to school with shared my honors classes, but most of my other buddies, those on the track team and those on the speed club, got funneled off into classes I never took. Being a nerd already distanced me from my nonacademic friends. I really didn't need space-age elitism widening the gulf.

Teenagers regard free congregation among their kind as a natural right and will sabotage or circumvent any segregation they don't impose themselves. We speed club members, separated from one another by our classes, reunited during lunch at a dining table in the cafeteria where skaters formed a shifting group between 11:30 and 1:00. We knew without being told not to bring non-skaters to our club area. The mood was generally mellow and good-humored as we forgot our tracks and related as skaters. For me though there was an exception.

Danny Swafford's lunch period overlapped mine and he was anything but a mellow lunch mate. If I was seated at the speed club table and he saw me, he'd bring his tray over and plop down next to me or across from me. "Hart," he'd say with a big smile. "Saw Katy last night. She said to say hi." In a conversational tone he'd proceed to narrate his latest carnal romp with my girlfriend. The Katy starring in his fantasies had a ravenous sexual appetite and less decorum than a monkey house. As Danny talked it became clear he spent way too much time pondering my girlfriend's pudenda. The orgies he described were ludicrous, but his well-crafted details sometimes struck home. Once he found out he could bug me with his wretched bullshit he never missed an opportunity to pass along news of his latest sexual extravaganza with my steady.

I wanted to shut him up, but I was reluctant to tell Katy the things he was saying about her because she might not believe me. Whenever Katy was around, Danny was the perfect gentleman.

The phony did everything but kneel and kiss her hand. I was still looking for a solution to my Danny problem when he intruded on my lunch yet again, bumping my tray with his as he smirked. "Hart, guess what!"

As he unwound the yarn of his latest debauchery with my girl I noticed he'd chosen meatloaf for his entrée. During my first two years at Roosevelt I'd eaten the cafeteria meatloaf often and had liked it, especially with ketchup. But eventually I got tired of the hard little somethings I occasionally bit into. Also, the grey, scrambled, anonymous texture of the ground beef appealed to me less over time. As I stared into the gestalt of Danny's mystery meat, I noticed a vague shape suggestive of a small rodent and got an idea. As innocently as I could I pointed with my fork. "Is that a mouse?"

Danny's mouth fell open. "No way!"

"Can't you see its tail?" I showed him helpfully. I really didn't expect him to fall for it but I could tell he had. Encouraged, I pointed out the mouse's haunch.

"I know, I know, I see it," he said. "Jesus! I think I ate its head!"

"I wouldn't worry. The oven killed any bacteria."

"Are you fucking *crazy*! I ate a *mouse's head*!"

"What are you going to do?"

"Goddamn cooks!" he yelled. "Let's see them talk their way out of this one!" He picked up his plate and went to complain.

I washed down the last of my four cinnamon rolls with chocolate milk and departed the cafeteria before he raised his stink. I didn't want to be identified as the discoverer of the mouse. I doubt the staff took Danny seriously but others did. That afternoon several of my friends asked me if I'd heard about the student who ate a ground-up mouse baked into his cafeteria meatloaf. I realized then that my improbable fib was one any junior high student would believe automatically—and I felt sorry for the cooks. The bad press I gave their hard-to-read protein product no doubt discouraged its consumption. But for one afternoon at least I shut Danny up.

SIXTEEN

DANNY Swafford's older brother Phil, sixteen, was about six-two. His girlfriend Lindy Decker, fourteen, was maybe five-two. When they free skated together Phil hunched down to bring his head closer to her level and although this was a thoughtful gesture his pronounced stoop made him look a little sneaky. Under the mirror ball, Lindy and her man competed with Gloria and Luke for the title of lovers most thoroughly entwined. Sometimes Phil escorted Lindy high in the bleachers where in the starlight they took things a bit further. They were rarely alone up there. Making out in the upper bleachers was a hallowed rink tradition.

Phil, like many of us, was fighting a protracted war with pimples—yet he was an attractive guy with a lean face and strong features, his nose perhaps a bit too strong. Lindy was a timid girl with short, curly orange hair and round blue eyes that protruded slightly. The scarlet lipstick on her full lips emphasized the brightness of her lovely smile, her most endearing feature and one we saw often because Lindy was in love. She idolized her man. There was evidence he loved her too. He spent whole sessions in her company, bought her cokes and potato chips, listened to hours of her bubbly chatter.

They'd been going together about a year when Lindy got pregnant. I learned about it from Katy, who was a good friend of Lindy's. At first it looked like everything would work out. Phil admitted he was the father and promised to marry Lindy, and that's what she said she wanted. Several weeks passed as the wedding plans lay dormant. Meanwhile Phil was giving Lindy one excuse after another. Then he stopped calling her and began avoiding the rink.

During a free skate one night I saw her sitting on a bench by the rail gazing into space. I rolled to her through the crowd. She was in her socks, with skates on one side of her and shoes on the other, so I couldn't tell whether she was coming or going. She looked like she might not know either. Her eyes were red and washed out, her pink fingernails chewed ragged. But as we traded small talk for a few minutes her downturned mouth lifted into a resigned smile. Then she slipped on her loafers and departed, carrying her skates.

Months later, during Christmas vacation, our family drove down to Oklahoma and spent a day with Mom's brother and his family in Bartlesville. John and I accompanied our Cousin Brent to the supermarket and in the parking lot we saw Lindy getting in a car with a big bump under her coat. Either she didn't see us or pretended she didn't. I figured she'd come south to finish her pregnancy far from curious eyes and would put the baby up for adoption. That seemed like the right choice to me. Lindy was too young to start a family by herself.

She never came back to the rink, not that I know. Phil came back and was his old fun-loving self, acting like nothing had happened. Everyone else acted like nothing had happened too. But I'm sure they had their opinions, as I had mine. I thought Phil stuck Lindy with all the responsibility for something they did together, using her in a very hurtful way. I was less friendly toward him after that and told myself I'd never run out on a girl like he did, even if I didn't love her. I was very sure of that.

Lindy's pregnancy made me consider the possibility of Katy getting pregnant. Our meltdown together in the easy chair had shown me what might happen. Was it time to take precautions? A teammate a year younger than me, Jimmy Brown, was in the habit of making out with his girlfriend in her apartment while her mother waitressed. He once showed me the rubber he carried in his wallet, just in case. It didn't have a wrapper and was rolled up inside itself, looking like a little beige beret. I could have followed his example, but I didn't, for several reasons. I thought if I tried to buy a rubber in a drugstore I'd probably get busted, or at least bawled out, because sale to a minor was illegal. Also Jimmy's rubber made a recognizable bump in his wallet, a bump I wanted to avoid in my wallet. I could of course carry my little friend in my jeans pocket, but what if I forgot and left it there and Mom found it when she did the wash? Or what if Katy spied its round contour showing through my pants and realized what it was? Would she think I was looking out for us or would she be convinced I had only one thing on my mind? It seemed easier, and safer, to wait until *she* wanted me to have a rubber. By then maybe I'd know how to get one.

SEVENTEEN

WHEN we were five, Jackie Dumond informed me we were going to get married when we grew up. I wasn't as sure of that as she was but it sounded okay. Certainly I liked her. During those early years of my life she was one of my best buddies, if not the best—a tomboy with a nose for adventure and more courage than all but a couple of my guy friends.

The Dumonds were part of our lives from as far back as I can remember. They lived across the street from our big white two-story frame house on the corner of Chautauqua and Gilbert. Theirs was a smaller, newer home in our middle class neighborhood overrun with postwar children. Our parents were friends and so were we four kids, especially Jacqueline and me. Jackie's psychologist father believed in nearly unlimited childhood freedom and, predictably I think, his belief was put to the test. Jackie's older brother, given a new Schwinn bicycle for his birthday, dedicated himself to its destruction just to disprove the company's claim that its bike was indestructible. It took him two days. He rode the beautiful, expensive and nearly indestructible machine over curbs and off walls, pushing himself until he crumpled a rim and bent the fork. His punishment: no replacement bike. His sister Jackie, though not aggressive, was an equivalent handful, burning with a bright and confident spirit perhaps over-nurtured by her pop. She seemed to lack most human fears—and any trace of a superego.

When Jackie and I were seven we ran away from home together—she because her mother told her no, me because Jackie's plan to set up in the wilderness far from parental supervision sounded like a hoot. The wagon next to her was loaded with camping gear and grub so I knew we were well provisioned. We took turns pulling the wagon as we trekked by sidewalk two blocks south and across Lincoln Street to the recently bulldozed acreage where a new city park was in the early stages of development. There in the wild we pitched our bedsheet tent next to a rain puddle lake. We were building a real campfire with construction debris to heat our baked beans and toast our marshmallows when our mothers arrived in a car. Under maternal guidance I put my pants back on and Jackie her dress. We'd thoughtfully stripped down to our undies before swimming in the lake and getting muddy.

When we were eight, Jackie invited me over to try her new sack swing suspended from a high limb in her backyard. She led me up a ladder and onto their garage roof, where two or three older kids sat waiting in line ahead of us, trying not to slide down the incline. The idea was to catch the gunnysack packed with newspapers as it swung up within reach, hop aboard and ride it down almost to the lawn then high up over peony bushes. The guy ahead of me got in eight or ten long swings before he dismounted and dropped to the grass. Then it was my turn and as my ride rose toward me, I foolishly looked down, learning with a shock how surprisingly far I was from dear Mother Earth. I lost confidence and wanted to wait until I knew what I was doing but Jackie's "Go! Go!" spurred me on. Blindly I dove for the departing sack, barely touching it before crashing onto the lawn with outstretched arms. I managed to break the fall, but also my left wrist. It was my first trip to the emergency room, where the bones were set and my arm encased in a heavy, scratchy plaster cast from thumb to elbow.

Little Jacqueline was quite cute, with big blue eyes and a heart-shaped face below dark bangs cut straight as a ruler. An impertinent smile often exposed her extremely even teeth. Grinning like the Cheshire cat she would tell my mother whoppers—the many reasons why she could *not* have broken that flowerpot or how pirates pillaged her house and tied up her mom. Jackie's bald-faced lies, especially the self-serving ones, drove my mother up the wall. After my friend went home she rolled her eyes and in an amusing falsetto mimicked Jackie telling a preposterous falsehood.

When Jackie was about ten, her parents bought a hundred-acre farm north of town, a long property that hugged the east bank of the Arkansas River. After the Dumonds moved, our families visited back and forth and sometimes John and I stayed overnight on the farm. One of these overnighters happened when Jackie and I were in ninth grade. I hadn't seen her for a couple of years and found her at age fifteen trim and tan and dressed in jeans and a cotton print blouse, a tomboy becoming a pretty teen. As always when we visited, Jackie gave John and me a tour to show us what was new.

She drove us on her Dad's tractor to a seldom-traveled lane on the eastern boundary of their property where she and a neighbor boy had built an impressive treehouse. It was a two-story fortress composed of dismantled packing crates and set into an Osage orange hedgerow. The treehouse base was about ten feet off the ground and there were four rooms, two upstairs and two down, all furnished with castoffs—worn throw rugs, a shaky card table and folding chairs, cabinets, a bookcase, and an old mattress. Each room had a big window with a shutter that could be lifted and fastened to the ceiling, providing a cinematic view of the dirt road below and the field beyond. It was all very nice, but as I considered the feeling of domesticity in that arboreal crib, I developed an unsettling suspicion about that old mattress. My suspicion grew when Jackie said she and Wayne, her fellow builder, had formed a two-member club that met until her parents shut it down. I waited for her to explain why her parents did that, and when she didn't, I thought again about that mattress.

I'd met Wayne on previous visits. He was a friendly, uncomplicated guy and my replacement as Jackie's neighborhood pal. Now it looked like they were more than pals. As I considered her intrepid boldness, and his hormone-infused maleness, and their remote treehouse accessible only by rope ladder, I figured they'd crossed boundaries together. Jackie talked over and under and around the matter, giving me the feeling she was trying to let me know what had happened while keeping it from my brother.

She drove us next to the farm's western boundary, the Big Arkansas River, where a large-scale natural event was unfolding. A generation of carp was tooling downstream, a seemingly endless flow of two and three pound fish. Dorsal fins broke the surface all the way across the river and Jackie said it had been going on for days. Sitting on a sandbar next to the migration we took off our shoes and socks and rolled up our jeans. We waded into the current with Jackie leading. She cut through the water with her knees while smiling a slight smile I couldn't interpret. The way wet denim clung to her hips, showing the seams of her panties, caught my attention—and I thought again about that mattress. Carp were bumping our legs as they motored forward, driven by their shared instinct. They were programmed and dopey, easy to catch and hold. Two hundred yards upriver from us three teens standing in the current were filling gunnysacks with the defenseless fish for some purpose I couldn't fathom. We were most of the way to the other bank when we ran into the main channel, too deep to wade, and turned back.

After supper, Jackie, John and I ate our ice cream apart from her parents in the Dumond rec room. To my surprise and I imagine to my brother's surprise Jackie began salting her speech with gratuitous profanities, nothing shocking, just the basics like hell and damn and shit. Since I'd never heard her swear before, I wondered—why now? Then I realized it was another way of telling me she was growing up. A few minutes later her cussing ended as abruptly as it had begun.

Before bed the three of us for the first time took baths in two shifts, male and female. Previously we'd all scrubbed down in the tub together. When we were clean and free of river smell we dried off and put on pajamas and crawled into Jackie's oversized double bed just as we'd done when she and I were ten. Jackie chose the middle position, placing herself within inches of me. I began getting ideas and wondered if this was what she'd been prepping me for. I knew my brother would soon fall asleep, and even if he didn't I thought he'd pretend to be asleep if anything happened. I expected Jackie to stay awake, hoping for something to happen. Her bedroom was on the second floor, a long way in that rambling ranch house from the master bedroom on the first floor where her parents slept. Jackie's brother was staying over with a friend that night.

Later I heard John snoring lightly. Jackie lay on her side facing away from me and I doubted she was asleep. I thought she was probably waiting for me to make a move. All I had to do was lay my hand against her hip to show her I was interested, and then if she wanted to roll my way we could go from there. Yet I couldn't bring myself to do this simple thing. Actually it wasn't a simple thing. Jackie seemed to like me as much at fifteen as she had when we were kindergarteners, and I was afraid that if we had sex she'd want us to become a couple. I already had a girl-friend, one I loved, and something in Jackie's personality made it unlikely I'd ever care for her as much. Her apparent unshakable certainty about almost everything somehow undermined my own confidence. I think it's why I blindly jumped off her garage— listening to her instead of myself. In her bed that night I was conflicted though. She was so close and seemed so willing. I remembered the way she looked in wet jeans and thought how easy it would be, once we were kissing, to slide my hand under the elastic waistband of her pajama bottoms. I lay awake for an hour trying to decide whether to touch her or not. Finally, still undecided, I fell asleep.

I used to wonder why Jackie's parents let their daughter share a bed with me chaperoned only by my younger brother, a watch- man more interested in witnessing sex than in reporting it to the authorities. The Dumonds knew Jackie liked me. They knew she'd become sexually active. Surely they guessed she'd be ready for a little fooling around if I was. Why risk us knocking her up in the middle of ninth grade?

Jackie's parents were bright, responsible adults and over time I believe I figured out what they were thinking. When they learned about their daughter's club with Wayne they must have fixed her up with a contraceptive, in those days probably a diaphragm. Her dad's commitment to her freedom would seem to argue for nothing less. Once Jackie was equipped, her club with Wayne presumably could have reconvened, but I doubt it did. Wayne was from a single-parent family of very modest means. He wasn't headed for college like Jackie and me. I'd guess Jackie's parents worried that a deep relationship with him might lead to a less rosy future for their kid than they hoped for.

My family was as solidly middle class as Jackie's, and her par- ents liked my parents a lot. They also liked me. The prospect of Jackie forming a new club with the boy she'd once proposed to might sit well with them, and if that was their wish, they almost got it. Had Jacqueline been wearing sexier PJs that night or cologne as confusing as Katy's, I might have slipped.

EIGHTEEN

AROUND Christmas Katy's mother moved with her kids into her new boyfriend's place. He was a realtor about fifteen years older than Charlotte, a tall man with a long nose who wore a dark blue double-breasted suit and smelled of talcum. I only saw him once and he seemed pleasant enough. "He's teaching my mom real estate so she can get her license," is how Katy explained him.

The move meant a change of schools for Katy and Greg, usually not a good thing but there seemed to be a plus in Katy's case because she would begin attending my junior high. I imagined how it would be. Before first bell we'd hang out in her homeroom or mine. If our lunch periods overlapped we'd eat together at the speed club table—or better yet at our own table. I'd introduce her to all my friends. I was proud of Katy and wanted everyone to know we were a couple. I thought I'd be helping her fit in at her new school.

During her first week at Roosevelt I decided to surprise her. She'd told me her home room number so I climbed to the third floor and walked to the other end of the building. Down a short hallway I'd never visited before I found the room. I entered and scanned the faces and didn't see her. Was she late? I looked at the students again, more carefully, and this time I spotted her in a backrow seat in the corner of the room. Something was wrong with her. Apprehension clouded her face and she was trying to shrink into her desk. Her dress was one I'd never seen before. It was shapeless and way too young for her, a Horsey Girl dress whose drab green fabric drained away her color. She looked terribly vulnerable. I wanted to find out what was the matter but when I moved toward her she shook her head and waved me off, looking frightened. Obviously she didn't want to talk to me. I thought she wanted me to leave, so I did. With a knot in my gut I walked back to my homeroom hurt and confused. What did this mean for us as a couple? My girlfriend all of a sudden didn't want to know me.

At the Alaskan later in the week she pretended nothing had happened. She was back to her old self in every way, as though by putting wheels on her feet she'd regained her personality. Actually, I think that's about what happened. She was a star at the rink, allowing her to be confident, the Katy I was used to. I was glad to have her back but remained puzzled by what had happened at school. I knew better than to bring it up though. It was enough that we had a place to be together and that her feelings toward me hadn't changed. I didn't have to see her at school.

I've speculated many times about what Katy might have been thinking that day in her homeroom, cowering at her desk, the student farthest from the teacher and as far as possible from the other students. Her clothing, perfect for disappearing into any background, said it all. She didn't want to make friends or even to know anyone in that room. Her life, so different from mine, dictated that she *not* get acquainted at the new school because in a year or two she'd be transferring to another new school. She was opting out. Far from wanting to fit in at Roosevelt, she was trying slip through, anonymous and unremembered, a lovely ghost disguised as a wallflower.

Katy's situation was sad enough that I might have felt sorry for her if she'd been weak. But she wasn't weak. She was a person with strong feelings who'd been put through an emotional wringer, leaving her bruised and wary and tough. All the Linsey kids were like that. I think their strength came partly from their experiences and partly from their father, a guy I saw just once for maybe ten minutes. He was short and slightly built and had curly red hair. His blue eyes were serious but also relaxed and ready to laugh. When he smiled his brow furrowed so that his whole face seemed to be smiling. I don't think we spoke after greeting each other, but I liked the way he looked at me—friendly and curious rather than suspicious. I hoped to hell he couldn't see into my least presentable thoughts about his younger daughter. We were in the Alaskan parking lot with several of the older male speed skaters, and the high respect they had for Mr. Linsey was clear. It showed in their body language and in the gentle way they kidded around with him. They treated him as an honorary member of their group. I wasn't comfortable matching wisecracks with witty older guys so I played my familiar role of silent observer as Mr. L charmed an appreciative audience.

I can't think of anyone who didn't like Katy's dad. Certainly we all respected his military service. From books I knew that the US Marines had done some of the most difficult and courageous fighting of World War Two in the Pacific Islands where he'd served. He was too small and too modestly developed to fit my idea of a Marine, and for that reason I thought he must have guts beyond belief. Katy and I never talked about him but I'm pretty sure he was the grownup who most helped her develop the spine she needed to live her Tilt-A-Whirl life so productively. Mr. Linsey's obituaries were published not long ago and in them several people praise him for his positive, *saving* influence on his children.

NINETEEN

THOSE who entered the Alaskan during the last two weeks of December encountered a tall and fully decorated evergreen with blinking lights. Crepe paper strips spanned the rink lobby up high and holly wreaths hung on the walls. Inside the auditorium the H-beams supporting the roof were wound like barbers' poles with red and green crepe paper strips. Above the skating floor stretched holiday banners hung with golden paper bells. Songs of the season, both traditional and rock, invaded our DJ's playlist where they would remain until January 2nd, when Alvin and the Chipmunks and "I Saw Mommy Kissing Santa Claus" had begun to grate.

Christmas Eve each year featured a big feast for the Alaskan's two skating teams and their parents. The rink owners provided a roast turkey and a baked ham and the parents brought the rest. Laid out on tables were dressings for the turkey, assorted casseroles, bowls of mashed potatoes, green beans, candied yams, cranberry sauce, assorted fruit salads, and gelatins. There were apple pies and mince pies, cookies and a cake or two. The dinner usually kicked off a couple of hours before the night session. People loaded paper plates and carried them into the lower bleachers to eat. When the session began the leftovers stayed in place so the general public could share in the holiday eats. Speed club members whose home celebrations were slim made up for it by revisiting the food until the turkey and ham had been carved to the bone and the pie tins scraped clean.

On Christmas Eve the Alaskan drew its second largest crowd of the year. The largest crowd arrived on New Year's Eve. That night the rink was crammed with people, including many novice skaters and a fair number of first timers. The crowd's density and its low skating competence made traffic flow around the oval lethargic and herd-like. Our younger speed club members would have found that frustrating had they not cleverly turned the congestion into fun. They raced each other or played tag, flagrantly violating the speed limit as they threaded their way with ungracious finesse through the wobbling human deadwood. Stan Preboth's whistle blew more often on New Year's Eve than in an ordinary week but with little result. Stan was at a heavy disadvantage because between him and the violators rolled many delicately balanced bodies, ready to go down wind-milling into a heap if bumped or startled or, sometimes, just glanced at.

While circling the floor during these special sessions I would occasionally encounter a sweet and tangy aroma rolling off this or that adult skater, a smell I couldn't identify because my parents didn't drink. By keeping my eyes open I learned that some celebrants of Christ's birth had bottles stashed in their coats up in the bleachers. And at the end of the exit tunnel, where a portable exhaust fan was pushing heat and smoke into a frigid night, the seated door guard had a pint of bourbon concealed in the pocket of his khaki parka. Shots were available to friends on request.

The holiday sessions offered some exotic special skates not available on other nights of the year. Stan emceed a limbo competition, introducing the contestants and commenting briefly on performances. To a skater stalled under the bar he might say, "Heck of a place to run out of gas, Cory." On my first viewing of this contest I expected to be aggravated by a challenge so back-assward it stood the high jump on its head. However, as the bar descended from eighteen inches to fifteen then to twelve, I got drawn in. I had to admit it took skill to squeak under such a low height. Early in the competition most entrants rolled toward the bar on a perpendicular, sitting on one skate with their other skate thrust straight forward. Their challenge was to maneuver their upraised knees under the bar, and they all self-eliminated early. The finalists had highly personal styles—all of them weird. The winner during my time was a preteen girl built like a collapsible walking stick. With the bar set barely higher than her skate tops she took a full minute to pass under, inching forward in a tight arc as she lowered one bent limb after another.

When Katy and I joined the conga line we had to talk each other into it, probably because we were both afraid of looking bad. We dithered so long we became the last two links in the chain. I held Katy's hips as we were yanked into a stirring ride, slung this way and that and finally whipped off across the floor holding each other up. Laughing we raced for the end of the line and reattached and got thrown again.

As midnight approached on New Year's Eve, Stan announced the last skate of 1959 and Katy and I took the floor with the other lovers of all ages. It was my first changing of the year away from my family and my first in the company of a girlfriend. As I thought back over the preceding twelve months I realized a lot had happened in my life, most of it because of roller skating and Katy. Stan began the countdown over the PA and the crowd joined in. Noisemakers distributed earlier rattled and tooted and buzzed. At midnight "Auld Lang Syne" poured from the speakers and streamers flew from the bleachers through falling confetti. I turned around and skated backward in front of Katy so we could kiss. We held our kiss and each other as we rolled into the 1960s.

TWENTY

URING the school year some of us brought textbooks to the weeknight sessions, telling ourselves the rink was as good a place to study as any. In fact, it wasn't. I couldn't successfully tackle anything difficult there. The music alone prevented it because if I liked a song I found myself listening—and if I didn't like a song it became so annoying I couldn't focus on my work. Only my reading assignments for English drew me in enough to overcome the many rink distractions.

My ninth grade honors English teacher, Mrs. Yeoman, was one of my best teachers ever. I loved the reader she picked for us, an anthology full of unpretentious and involving short stories aimed at a broad audience rather than English majors only. Anyone fond of good, clear writing would have liked that book. I read stories in it that weren't assigned just because of the way they began. The one I remember best was narrated by the mother of a high school point guard. Mom watches his basketball team play a rival while she reports to the reader on the abuse he's suffering from the boy guarding him. He's being tripped and shoved and plowed into and the officials are missing half the fouls. She worries he'll be hurt.

Her son's team wins and in the game's aftermath the mother

sees him talking to the bully who roughed him up. She's puzzled because the conversation appears friendly. The two boys actually seem to like each other! Later, when she has her son alone, she asks him how he can be nice to someone who tried so hard to hurt him, and he tells her she doesn't understand. The boy guarding him played a clean game and that's one reason his team lost. The mother learns then that her cherished one is a talented "flopper," valued primarily for the bag of dirty tricks he uses to foul out an opposing team's best guard. She's a little shocked by the pride he takes in his underhanded but fruitful work. Whether he should be proud, or ashamed, along with a host of other issues including the nature of athletic competition and the ability of a mother to know her own child are left for the reader to think about. I'll bet most guys at Roosevelt would have liked that story and probably most girls. I remain grateful to our teacher for picking such an appealing text when stuffier, "more challenging" choices were available (aren't they always?).

For me, the high point of Mrs. Yeoman's class came when she gave us the option of writing a poem in place of a required essay. I worked hard on my poem about Abraham Lincoln, revising many times. My teacher liked it enough that she submitted it to the *NEA Journal* for a page containing student work. Although the editor there rejected it, I got my first taste of doing what writers do. Later, after I'd begun calling myself a writer, I found that poem and saw what I think Mrs. Yeoman liked about it. Although it was as simple as a glass of water, the sound and rhythm worked well and the emotion was genuine.

At least two skaters took textbooks to the rink for nonacademic purposes. Rick Shafer's sister Rachel and her friend Lauren McCabe, both of whom Katy disliked, at some point began doing math homework at the Alaskan. From out on the floor I'd see them seated low in the bleachers next to the rear exit tunnel, their texts open on their laps as they calculated on notebook paper with pencils. Inevitably, it seemed, one or the other would hit a trouble spot and when that happened I'd get flagged down. I was ahead of both girls in the math sequence so their problems were easy for me and I enjoyed playing the brain for such friendly and attentive scholars.

Maybe I should have been more aware that my tutees were two of the cutest girls at the rink in our age group. It was Katy who brought this to my attention. While I'd been cruising along blissfully in my role as mobile math tutor, she'd apparently been gathering evidence against her straying boyfriend. She was just as jealous and hot-tempered as I was and would disturb my tutorials by skating up and tossing me my name bracelet. Or she'd wait till I skated back to her, when she'd hold the bracelet out to me pinched between two fingers and dangling, like something she'd have preferred not to touch. Once again we'd be finished forever.

In my role as tutor I found a way to counter Katy when she flirted. And there wasn't a lot she could do about it. Only an absurdly possessive girlfriend would actually forbid me to pursue such an altruistic educational mission. And so it came about that while Katy flirted, I tutored. We trapped ourselves in a nonproductive cycle either of us could set in motion, butting heads and splitting up and reuniting sometimes two or three times a month. We were so devoted to our performances we barely noticed that other people were engineering some of them, maybe just to watch the fireworks.

TWENTY-ONE

ROM as far back as I can remember I could outrun all the boys my age and often boys older. I went undefeated through eighth grade and probably—well, wait a minute. Now that I think of it, that's not quite right. There was that time my third grade teacher, Miss Edgington, matched me up with a female classmate and we ran on the playground with the whole class watching.

I didn't want to do it. I thought, what glory can there be in beating a girl who's smaller than you and wears glasses? I'm going to look like a bully, aren't I? I did it only because my rep was on the line. When you're the fastest you have to give every challenger a shot at the title, however ridiculous the challenge.

My memory of that day has dimmed with the years but I seem to recall my foot slipping on the start. Then I remember vividly Ursula Ann Rimer's brown and white saddle shoes pounding the turf a yard or two ahead of me to the bitter end. As she and I walked back to our group, I noticed everyone looking at us, the winner and the loser. Among my male classmates several mouths hung open. The girls and our teacher smiled quietly. And I knew I'd been had.

My next organized competition came in spring of ninth grade

when I tried out for my junior high track team. On the afternoon of tryouts a required meeting made me late for practice. I finally walked down to the playing field in my gym clothes an hour late and handed Assistant Track Coach Lester my permission slip from the Safety Club, a club I'd been pressured into joining. Coach smiled at me. "Safety Club?" I realized he'd just identified the most wimpy pantywaist among his track hopefuls.

"A teacher volunteered me."

"You couldn't miss one day?"

"They elected me president. I thought I had to be there."

"The time trials are over, Hart. Sorry."

As I stood there devastated, not knowing what to say, Head Track Coach Butterworth diplomatically took me aside and timed me doing the 50, the 100, the 220 and the 330 with just enough time between to catch my breath. In every race I used the same strategy, running as hard as I could all the way. I thought I'd done okay in the three shorter races but knew I'd faded badly at the end of the 330.

Before we rejoined the team Coach Butterworth mentioned matter-of-factly that my times were best in all four events. The news went straight to my head where it began ginning up a day-dream production machine starved for fodder. I was so high on me I forgot to consider that for the previous year I'd been training as a speed skater. Of course I did well in the time trials. I was in the best shape of my life.

At the beginning of practice the next day I was warming up with Dave Lankford, my main competition on the team in the 50 and the 100. We were doing wind sprints on the greening athletic field and moving at a pretty good clip. Apparently that wasn't enough for me. Drunk on the wine of my trial times, I wanted more challenge and began speeding up. Dave hung with me until soon we were both turning over near capacity. Knowing I had more top end, I shifted into overdrive and started pulling away.

Dave realized he was beaten and slowed. I was flying over the clover, relishing my victory, when searing pain flared in my right groin and I immediately lost power. In one desperate stride my sprint became a hobble and I stumbled and almost went down. I limped to a stop, knowing I'd screwed up my leg.

Dave was walking toward me. "What happened?"

"Think I pulled a muscle." I'd never done that before, but I'd heard about muscle pulls and my injury felt like what I'd heard—debilitating weakness and a lot of pain. I told Coach Butterworth what had happened and he said it sounded like a pulled muscle to him. Coach Lester eyed me with mild disgust. "Might as well pack it in, Hart. Grab a shower and take off." My walk home that evening was painful but at least I could walk. What I couldn't do was run. I know because I tried.

My parents reacted to the crisis in their usual manner—they looked for a solution. They drove me to a clinic near College Hill Park where the medical staff confirmed I'd torn muscles in my right groin. I was prescribed hot whirlpool baths in their rehab room and applications of an electric heating pad to the injured groin. Everyone was so professional I became quite hopeful, but when after five or six visits I could detect no improvement, I abandoned the heat treatments, wet and dry, of Western medicine.

My parents then suggested a chiropractor. Neither of them had ever been to one but they'd gotten a tip from friends. I was willing to try anything that might work. My first visit to Dr. Bosman in his storefront office began with him taking several full body X-rays as I lay in different positions on a calibrated grid. While zapping me he asked about my treatments at the clinic. "The doctors there couldn't help you?"

"Not really."

"Why am I not surprised?" he said with a wry smile. "Those wunderkind know just enough about the human skeleton to set a bone." Together we looked at my X-rays while he interpreted, using his retractable pen for a pointer. He showed me that my right leg was nearly an inch and a half longer than my left, something I wasn't able to observe in the exposures but that I thought might be true because I tend to stand with my right knee bent, as though there's too much leg on that side. According to Dr. Bosman, this mismatch threw my pelvis out of balance, stressing muscles in the right groin. Professional manipulation was needed to loosen my frame and adjust my pelvic alignment.

He had me take off my shirt and stretch out face down on his leather-encased chiropractic table. Then he manipulated me from stem to stern, popping I think every joint in my body. His parting shot was to grip my skull in his sinewy fingers and manipulate that, getting a tiny pop out of my cranium—though it may have been one of his knuckles. Hearing and feeling my bones being liberated from their bad habits was wonderfully relaxing. On my walk home the pain in my groin was much reduced. Encouraged, I tried to run and managed a fast lope. Great, I thought. Just one chiropractic visit and already I'm half healed. At practice the next day I told Coach Butterworth the good news and he asked when I'd be ready to compete. "Two weeks," I said with confidence. On that basis he entered me for our first meet in the 100, the 220, and the 4X220 relay.

My recovery turned out to be much slower than I'd supposed. After each appointment with the doctor I felt great for a day or two, then my bones would gradually backslide into their bad habits, falling out of alignment to restress the injury and reawaken the pain. Nevertheless, I *was* slowly getting better. A week before the meet I began practicing handoffs with our relay team and could match speeds with both my handoff partners. I'm going to be able to do this, I thought.

The meet was with Robinson and my first event was the 220. I knew I needed to go easy on the start to protect the pull, even if I fell behind. I reminded myself I had an eighth of a mile to catch up. As race time approached adrenalin entering my blood brought that pervasive nervousness known as "butterflies." My jitters multiplied until by the time I waited on my fingertips for the gun, I was so hopped up I completely forgot my plans for caution and reverted to habit at the crack of the pistol. I blasted off like I'd been goosed by the Great Cosmic Finger. As I jumped into the lead my groin blazed with pain, quickly shutting me down. I limped off the track, cursing myself for tearing the same muscles all over again.

The coaches scratched me in the 100 but left me on the relay, probably because it was too late to replace me. Our event came late in the meet so I had some time to recover. On the eve of our event I practiced my handoff with Gary Gunter on the infield and learned that if I built speed slowly I'd probably be fine. During the race, once I took the baton I eased into a fast stride and cruised, adding steadily to the big lead our first two legs had built over Robinson. Gary brought it home and we won by almost half a lap in a two-lap race. This would be the lone highlight of my track season. The coaches didn't enter me in the meets that followed and I didn't blame them. I'd proved I wasn't reliable.

At the Wichita junior high track and field championships in May, Dave Lankford, the guy I'd outrun when I hurt myself, won the 50-yard dash. Many of my other teammates medaled as well. The team celebrated with a dinner at a buffet restaurant where I feasted on roast chicken, mashed potatoes, and coleslaw—feeling like a fraud. Happy teammates all around me had helped Roosevelt win the team title. I'd just pulled a muscle.

TWENTY-TWO

ARLY that spring all ninth graders at Roosevelt were given a job preference test. We were told it could predict the sort of work that might best suit us as adults. I was skeptical that a machine-scored exam could predict my future career better than I could, even though I knew I was in the dark about that. My parents had made me so secure that I'd felt no need to think seriously about my career, so I hadn't. They believed I'd make a good attorney—and being an attorney sounded okay to me. As I saw it, I'd pull in enough bucks to live the way I wanted and would get respect. That's why when people asked what I was going to be, I usually said "a lawyer." But I knew my answer was basically a façade. I hoped the test might point me to some field I hadn't yet considered, one that really grabbed me.

The psychological pigeonholing device consisted of about a hundred questions, all of which asked me to make a choice between two different activities. They read like this: "Would you rather (a) write a letter to a friend or (b) plant a tree?" I answered as honestly as I could though sometimes it wasn't easy. There was a lot of redundancy built into the exam and I felt more than once that I might be going against a choice I'd made earlier. It also bothered me that I was tending to choose outdoor pursuits in nature over indoor pursuits among people. While I liked fishing in the woods, I really didn't think I wanted a career with the National Park Service. We were not told how or when we'd learn the test results.

Near semester's end, we ninth graders were encouraged to sign up for appointments with Mr. Sondergard, Roosevelt's guidance counselor. Here it is, I thought. He's going to tell us how that test read our vocational tea leaves. The appointments were in the evening and we could come alone or bring our parents. My mother and father wanted to go of course. Katy's parents were busy, so she signed up for the conference after mine and we gave her a ride. I was a little surprised she wanted an appointment. She and I had never discussed careers and I'd assumed she didn't have one in mind. On the trip to Roosevelt, though, she seemed upbeat and bright with anticipation—more so than me. When I asked her about it she admitted she wanted to know the test results but wouldn't tell me what career she was interested in. I knew not to push.

Mr. Sondergard welcomed my parents and me into his office and offered us seats. He settled in behind his desk and began complimenting me on my fine record at Roosevelt. Using too many words he said that based on my grades and my standardized test scores and the comments of my teachers, I could be "anything I wanted to be." Just the kind of praise parents love to hear and a glance at my mother's face told me she'd heard. Dad looked pleased too. And why not? His son could be anything he wanted: doctor, lawyer, merchant, chief, physicist, cop, bouncer, thief—anything at all! Not long after that Mr. Sondergard ushered us out of his office and that's when I realized he wasn't going to tell me the results of the job preference test. Nor had we discussed careers in any meaningful way. What exactly had been the reason for the conference—or for the test?

A glorious prairie sunset was fading to twilight over downtown as I waited in the car with my parents for Katy to return from her conference. When she climbed in the back seat and sat down next to me I saw her hopeful look was gone. She was in such a bad mood I knew better than to poke around in it. We rode in silence for a while, then she surprised me by asking what Mr. Sondergard had said to me.

"He said I can be anything I want."

"He didn't tell you what you'd be good at?"

"No."

"What else?"

"He congratulated me on my grades and stuff."

"That's all?"

I said it was. Then I asked what he'd said to her. She wouldn't tell me. Whatever it was had discouraged her enough that she'd decided to hold it balled up inside among the million other things she was holding inside. I was used to it. That was my Katy!

Over the years I've thought many times about that strange evening. Today it seems to me I must have put Mr. Sondergard in a difficult position. How could he explain to my parents and me that based on my test-determined interests I'd be happiest herding elk in Yellowstone? Given the values of the school system he represented, that would have been pretty much impossible. I think he took the safe route, blowing smoke while letting me figure out my career. Maybe he realized that no test or person could predict the future of such a quirky kid.

In Katy's case, it seems to me our counselor miscalculated simply because he knew too little about her. She wouldn't have signed up to see him if she hadn't aspired to a profession of some kind. Unfortunately he had only three ways to assess her ability to succeed at a profession—her B grades, her probably so-so test scores, and the evaluations of her teachers at Robinson, teachers he likely didn't know. Based on what he had, he must have assumed my girlfriend's intelligence and motivation were too pedestrian for the career her test results pointed to. The biggest strike against her would have been her gender. In 1960, girls weren't encouraged to think about careers. Far from it. Most of society, men and women too, thought ladies were best employed as "homemakers."

The Katy Linsey Mr. Sondergard didn't know, but that I knew, was a dedicated and focused competitor with a record of success. What made her a good racer, beyond athletic ability, was her strong motivation. It was in her nature to always try her hardest. I think she wanted to show everyone (including herself) that she could rise above any perceived shortcomings in her background and stand on her own accomplishments. Over the years I've noticed that personalities like hers usually do well in adult life. She likely would have thrived in any career she chose. I could certainly see her as a nurse, a profession wide open to women at the time.

My memories of that evening are among my saddest because I believe I witnessed one of the major defeats of Katy's life—the death of her career dream. Her family was not well off or super supportive like mine. She knew it was up to her to make something of herself and no doubt that's why by age fourteen she'd thought carefully about what she wanted to be. She'd picked her future career and had evidently set her heart on it, only to learn she lacked the right stuff to pursue it, at least according to our counselor.

Mr. Sondergard's aim in both our cases must have been to guide us onto the paths that would take us through high school and beyond. He steered me away from the Park Service by keeping me on the academic track that led through good colleges to the professions, much in line with the goals of the honors program. And I think he steered Katy, who was less academically promising but certainly pretty, onto the path travelled by future receptionists and secretaries. His advice to her wouldn't have mattered so much if my girlfriend had had other career guides. She had none that I know except her older sister, who was a teen herself, and her mother. Katy must have been left with a single, limiting map for her future. Being who she was, she would have followed that map earnestly and with a steady purpose into a vocation much different than she'd hoped for.

TWENTY-THREE

MEADOWLAKE was a privately owned swimming hole open to the public in farm country south of town. The manmade body of water with a bottom eighty feet deep had begun as a sandpit dredged by a local construction company. After the pit played out, a developer turned the property into a rustic water park by filling in a corner of the lake with sand and adding diving boards, swings, and a dock for boat rentals. It was one of the places we Alaskan skaters out of school for the summer got our kicks.

The coarse blond river sand composing Meadowlake's beach sloped gently to the water then descended underwater to a depth of about ten feet. The lake bottom remained at ten feet until fifty yards from shore where it plunged into the dark unfilled abyss. Above the drop-off a braided plastic rope strung with floats marked the line beyond which swimmers weren't allowed. A lifeguard seated on a tower blew his whistle at anyone who crossed the float line or rode the rope as I once did. Only canoes, paddleboats and the like were permitted in the deep water. If someone had gone under out there it would have taken a professional diver in a helmet to retrieve the body.

At the top of the beach stood a roughhewn one-story building painted brown. A concession stand occupied one end of it and two changing rooms the other. Mature elms grew behind the building and around the lake, screening us from the rest of the world except when workers at Boeing several miles to the east tested the B-52 engines. The horrendous rumbling of the giant thrusters bolted to mounts in a long hanger could be heard all over Wichita.

To get to Meadowlake we took K-15 into Wichita's southern outskirts, then turned onto a two-lane blacktop and later a dirt road passing under elms to a wooden shed where the ticket seller sat in the shade. The ticket girl I remember best was in her late teens and had an amazingly full chest only partly corralled by her low-cut cotton blouse. After we pulled up, she cruised toward us barefoot in cutoff jeans with her roll of tickets. Bending at the waist, she sold admission through our rolled-down windows while offering an eye-popping view of her hanging lovelies. For those interested in such things, it was a live peep show rolled into the price of admission.

I once witnessed the inadvertent upstaging of this soft-core performance. My brother and I were visiting Meadowlake with Steve Bertholf and his older sister Marlene, who was seventeen or eighteen. Marlene was model thin, though not model tall, and engrossingly pretty. Every day before she met the world she spent at least an hour perfecting her immaculate face with makeup. At night, after her date with her boyfriend, she spent another hour deconstructing her mask with cold cream, solvents and cotton balls. None of it was really necessary. Marlene was absolutely gorgeous with or without cosmetics.

On this day I happened to be sitting next to her in the front seat while she dug for money in a purse the size of a saddle bag. The ticket seller waited patiently, showcase on display. Then Marlene's moving arm buckled the top of her swimsuit and—lo and behold!—for just a second I witnessed surpassing beauty. It was a breast the size of a large thimble and exquisitely shaped. This unpretentious mammary was more arousing than the heavyweights deployed next to my ear, I think because, being mostly nipple, it looked so sensitive. Marlene, totally unaware, taught me just what I needed to know at exactly the right moment in my life. There are many ways for a woman's breast to be the stuff of dreams. Chairman Mao perhaps put it best when he wrote, "Let a thousand flowers bloom!"

Another afternoon I went to Meadowlake with Katy and our younger brothers. We rode with Luke and Gloria and it must have been a weekend because the place was packed and there were many more young adults than usual. This was the day I saw my girlfriend for the first time in a swimsuit—a modest blue nylon one-piece. I learned she was built like a diminutive Russian gymnast with smooth limbs.

Hot sand burning our feet moved Katy and me into the water, which was warm but got cooler the deeper we waded. At my suggestion we swam for the sunning raft where grownups were stretched out feeding their tans. Our strokes were equally lacking in style. Mine was a funky sidestroke my mother taught me, Katy's a primitive crawl that involved a lot of splashing.

At the raft, instead of joining the sunbathers, we clung to the side of the platform, hidden from the adults and in the shade. Katy's eyes in that light were cobalt and when I looked into them I felt we were looking straight into each other's minds. Never more in love with her, I knew a kiss was needed. Thinking we had privacy, I made it a long one. Later we swam underneath the platform and in the airspace between floating fifty-five gallon drums we kissed again. Though suitably clandestine, that spot lacked the right ambiance and we didn't stay long.

Back on shore we rented a paddleboat while our brothers rented a canoe. Greg mocked his sister and me with that old schoolyard taunt, "Bill and Katy sitting in a tree, K-I-S-S-I-N-G."

Apparently we hadn't been as discreet as I'd thought. With the little twerps rudely dissing the venerable laws of primogeniture by laughing at us, Katy and I cranked up our lumbering battleship and charged, frothing the lake with four hard-driving speed skater legs. Though we failed to ram the enemy vessel, we did learn that a canoe is much swifter and more maneuverable than a paddleboat and that a canoe paddle can't be beat for firing water hard and on target. Outgunned, and half-soaked, Katy and I surrendered.

Once an armistice was in place, the two crews fell into harmony and circumnavigated the lake as a team, looking for trouble. The closest we came was an apparently unattached couple whose air mattresses had somehow drifted together. She was lying on her back with her bikini top undone, pretending to be asleep, and he was lying on his back pretending to be asleep while peeking at the breasts only partially concealed by loose bikini cups. Up the leg of his swimsuit an emphatic signal of his appreciation stood at attention. This natural event, the business of two people and no one else, for some reason got Greg and John to giggling. The amorous couple pretended harder than ever to be asleep as we floated by.

In the evening we started home with the car windows down. The elms were full of shadows and the heat of the day was easing while a million cicadas buzzed in unison all around us. I sat in the backseat with my girlfriend and a brother or two feeling relaxed and pleasantly tired. Katy's hair was down and still damp as she combed out tangles, missing me with her elbow. I liked it when her hair, cool and smelling of coconut oil, brushed against me. I saw a touch of sunburn along the bridge of her lightly freckled nose. After the comb went back in her purse we held hands into the city until my brother and I got dropped off. It had been one of the happiest days Katy and I ever spent together.

TWENTY-FOUR

A young ape's progress toward manhood is sometimes interrupted by dismaying regressions. I experienced one that summer when the Duckwalls in our local shopping park began selling small plastic slingshots at a rock bottom price—ten cents I believe. They looked flimsy so I tested one by pulling back on its pocket. Its skinny arms bent toward me, threatening to snap. Not what I would normally look for in a slingshot but the price was right. It was worth a dime just for the novelty.

When I fired my new toy in our backyard it surprised me by flinging a rock the size of my thumbnail thirty or forty yards. Small but deadly was my little sling, like a derringer. I realized rocks would be too dangerous so I experimented with other ammo and learned the best easily available grew on two tall evergreen bushes at the end of our backyard. In the spring these bushes loaded up with hundreds of green seeds covered in soft spikes. Seeds the size of a marble made the best slugs, heavy enough to sting a leg through jeans but too soft to break skin or damage an eye. I practiced firing my organic bullets for a week, plugging trees and trash cans and spooking the squirrels. When my brother and Steve Bertholf saw me shooting up the landscape they bought their own dime slingshots and joined the training exercises.

At that point we needed an enemy. Since I saw us as an updated version of the Robin Hood band (outlaws for justice), our opponents had to be worthy—richly deserving of punishment and threatening enough to even the stakes between hunters and hunted. The answer was obvious, to me at least. When I was in fourth grade, a sedan trying to beat a yellow light had almost wiped me out. If a friend hadn't grabbed me, I'd have stepped off the curb in front of that car and likely died. The memory stamped itself on my brain as securely as my own name, and afterward I knew in my bones how easily and unexpectedly an automobile could put me in my grave.

A year or two later I was peddling home on my one-speed bicycle when a car barreling down a cross street failed to yield. Braking hard, I skidded to a stop as the driver, seemingly oblivious, streaked by a few feet in front of me. If I'd continued on, I think he would have hit me. That day I understood the danger of a speeder in a residential neighborhood.

Another time I was in our backyard when I heard plaintive whining. I followed the terrible sound to the intersection in front of our house where the neighbors' pet boxer lay with a broken hip. My canine buddy was lucky—he got a pin and survived the hit and run—but the violator who'd fled the scene was even luckier. He escaped punishment altogether. Bad drivers, I could see, were often immune to law enforcement.

Cars had convinced me they were fair game, and each of them contained one or more people who might jump out and come after us, intent on stomping our butts. Great! That meant we had to be brave to attack and clever to avoid capture. Engagement with the enemy would be easy. Every few minutes a four-wheeled marauder passed behind the head-high spirea bushes that fenced our yard along Gilbert Street. We hit only cars going east, which gave us better cover, and our punishment was strict but fair. Vehicles moving at what we judged a legal clip we let pass unmolested while speeders felt our firepower.

Our escape route followed a longstanding informal passage from the end of our backyard up the middle of the block. The developers who'd built our division decades earlier had provided accommodation for an alley by leaving open space behind each lot, but since that time many homeowners had extended wire fences beyond their rear property lines in a land grab. Kids before us had countered the encroachments by blazing a new passage along the old right of way, bending down the tops of two or three of the offending fences and cutting a hole in the bottom of another. The overgrown passageway through the dark heart of our neighborhood could be traveled swiftly by insiders but was hidden from others. It gave easy access to several backyards that provided good cover for hiding.

During our first ambush we watched our ammo ricochet off the street ten yards behind the speeding car. It took several vehicles for us to figure out how much to lead by, but eventually we listened with satisfaction as our green bullets thunked into side panels and thwacked closed windows. If a driver slowed after being hit, I took no chances. I led the squad from our backyard over the Mennonite pastor's fence, through his wife's ferns, under the Graber's fence and down an aisle of weeds until we split up and hid in three backyards. I lay still and listened for the sound of pursuers crashing through the underbrush but all I ever heard were the faint sounds of citizens going about their days elsewhere in the city.

Our assaults were so much fun we wanted to share the joy. Robin Hood's expanding band, squatting behind the hedge, some with cocked slingshots and others with seeds in their hands, grew from three to five to seven and on some days eight or nine. The new troops were our friends from the neighborhood, school buddies, and Alaskan skaters. Eventually we stripped the evergreens of ammo and began substituting baby crabapples and mud balls. Our barrages now resembled jazz percussion riffs, loud and a little alarming, I would think, for those inside the cars. Our escape route worked so flawlessly I was lulled into believing we couldn't be touched.

On an afternoon when our hedge line was already crowded with troops, we were joined by two brothers from Chautauqua Street who had not yet slung for the hood. For purposes of disguise let's call these late additions to our posse Slowpoke and Snail. Their first target came fast, a big four-hole Buick piloted by a man with a lead foot. My dried mudball exploded on a fender among other hits all over the car and then I heard what I never had before—the banshee wail of tires stopping on a dime followed by a car door slamming shut.

Knowing we had a live one, I hurdled the pastor's fence, signaling to my men the need for maximum dispatch in retreat. The exodus began smoothly but I wasn't around to see the end of it and learned later what had happened. When the driver saw our rear guard, little Snail, struggling over the pastor's fence, he yelled, "Hey you! Hold it right there!" Snail, an obedient soul, froze in transit and submitted to capture. Seeing this, older brother Slowpoke, hidden in the ferns, stood up and let himself be taken.

I was lying facedown under a bush in somebody's backyard half a block away when I heard the driver yell. I waited quietly for fifteen minutes, listening for further information, and when none came I called out in a low voice to John and Steve, who'd been right behind me as we fled. Both answered from nearby. We walked out to Lorraine Street together and took it north several blocks into Steve's neighborhood. At his house we watched TV for a couple of hours, letting things cool down. Then, curious about what had happened at the scene of the crime, we walked back to our place.

When we turned the corner onto Chautauqua we saw the black and whites a block away. They were parked in front of our house, three cruisers and a station wagon. Several cops stood on our lawn watching us. Also watching us were two German shepherds on leashes with their ears up. Knowing it was pointless to run, we walked that long block into police custody. The authorities already knew our names and needed only to sort out which was which. The others busted that day—Slowpoke, Snail, and four of my school friends—had been processed and sent home. We all were given appointments for interviews at police headquarters downtown.

During my family's interview, a lieutenant explained that John and I now had arrests on our juvenile rap sheets, a serious matter. And yet, he said, if we avoided further violations until we turned eighteen, all public record of our arrests would be expunged. I felt guilty for getting my friends and brother in trouble, and for again disappointing my parents, but I didn't entirely regret the crime wave I'd fostered. As I saw it, we broke the law, but so did the speeders, and their infractions were a greater threat to the public welfare.

TWENTY-FIVE

I N June our rink hosted the 1960 RSROA speed skating championships for our Midwestern region. During the days leading up to the meet both of the Alaskan's rear door guards, armed with paint cans and brushes, repaired damage to the dark-green rubberized paint covering the rail and bleachers. Owner Clarence Hayes sanded the entire floor with a chest-high commercial machine that glided on a vibrating pad and left behind fine sawdust. Compacted chewing gum and soft drink stains melted away under the hustling sandpaper, providing a clean, hypersmooth surface for our races. Public sessions were cancelled for the weekend of competition and the rink marquee began announcing the championships.

On the first day of the meet my brother and I entered the rink for our heats and made our way through a lobby full of speed skaters in a colorful variety of club uniforms, all consisting of a long-sleeve jersey, cotton tights below the waist, and, over the tights, snug satin shorts. In the concessions area male veterans from our team were trading news and kidding around with veterans from visiting teams. There was a lot of comradery among these Senior Men (ages eighteen and up) despite the fact they would soon be competing for the same few medals. Some of the

Seniors from other clubs were in their thirties, older than any of our guys, and one of those was regular Army, on the staff at Fort Leonard Wood in Missouri. It struck me that many Seniors were small in stature with legs like hickory—and I wondered why.

John and I suited up in a dressing room, then climbed into the bleachers and watched heats. After the skaters in the race before mine cleared the floor, I made my way down to the oval and began warming up with those in my heat. Rosin powder was thick around the turns—the wood was white with it—yet Larry Lucas was adding more, shaking the powder can between his widespread skates as he rolled slowly through the curves. It was my dream floor, so tight my wheels squawked as I powered out of turns. For the first time I could use all my power without sliding out, a definite advantage and one I knew I might need because of my disadvantage. Track season had ended only a month earlier and my muscle pull was still on the mend.

My first heat was an 880. Coming off the starting line I remembered to protect my injury by running just fast enough to take the lead. Then I used the tight floor to pull away from those behind me, all but one guy I couldn't shake. Glancing back I saw it was my friend Rick, skating faster than I thought he could. He was drafting on me—and something else. In the straightaways I felt a hurricane of activity happening just to my rear though I couldn't see what it was. Rick stayed with me but didn't try to pass and we crossed the finish line first and second, far ahead of the others. I knew I'd just skated my fastest half mile.

I wanted to check out the rest of my competition so I hung around for the second heat of the Junior Men's 880. The skaters in that race were warming up when a massive hulk resembling the Jolly Green Giant without his hat rolled out of the lobby and onto the floor, seizing my attention and surely everyone else's. The muscular blond teen sprinted on his toe stops, getting up to speed, then meshed gracefully with those sailing around the oval. As he accelerated to pass the man ahead of him his massive thighs threatened to split the faded green tights of his under-funded Pueblo, Colorado speed club.

I remembered Richard Musso from the Greeley regionals a year earlier when he'd won our division. A guy that big you don't forget. I hadn't expected to face him again because I assumed he'd been bumped up to Intermediate Men, the division for sixteen and seventeen year olds. It didn't seem possible that a fifteen-year-old kid could be as big and buff as the average college line-backer of the day. He was half a foot taller than me and at least seventy pounds heavier. The only thing my age about him was his decidedly juvenile face—downy-cheeked, large-lipped, heavily freckled, and capped by a curly gold mop begging for a barber. As he tore around the oval making everyone else look small and sluggish, his curls blew back and shook. He had an unusual skating style, more erect than most, and when he powered out of turns he bowed his arms in front of him kind of like Superman, something I'd never seen a skater do. His wheels squawked joy-fully in the heavy powder as he fell in love with our floor. By race time everybody knew who would win.

Musso thundered off the starting line swinging his elbows and arrived at the first pylon with a two-yard lead. I imagined being up against him. I had a fast start too, so as we bore down on the first pylon I knew we'd come together. What if this upright rhinoceros clocked me in the face with a shrunken leather elbow pad? What if our skates got tangled—who'd be the one going down under the wheels of the other? For the first time since I started racing I felt physically intimidated by another skater. Musso built his lead steadily through seven laps and won by forty yards.

After lunch at home John and I returned to the rink mid-afternoon to compete in heats at our shorter distances. Posted on the lobby wall were the times for our morning heats. My 880 time was several seconds faster than my previous best, and, more to the point, only two tenths of a second slower than Musso's. It meant I had a chance against him. If I could beat him on the start, I figured the odds of winning would shift to me.

An hour later I was poised on my toe stops, leaning forward, right arm angled down, waiting for the start of my 440 heat—and worrying. I wasn't worried about my immediate competitors because I'd beaten all of them in the 880 we'd shared that morning. For some inexplicable reason I was worrying prematurely about how to beat Musso on the start when we matched up in finals *the next day*. Should I pick a spot on the line inside of him or outside of him? How fast could I afford to sprint on my hurt leg? How avoid his swinging elbows? Lost in my ill-timed speculations, I was caught flat footed by the starter's pistol as everyone else surged off the line. True to form, I panicked and scrambled in desperation for the first pylon. I managed to take the lead—but I also pulled the muscles in my groin *yet again*! This new tear burned like fire, yet because the race was short I was able to hold the lead until I rounded the last pylon. That's when Rick challenged, I think because he knew I was hurt. He almost got around me, losing by a foot or two. Afterward we circled the floor together, catching our breath, him happy, me pretending to be happy. I figured I'd just ended any chance I had of winning our division.

The next morning my leg burned every time I put weight on it. At the rink, as I joined the other 880 finalists warming up around the pylons, a blunt ache began to throb in the middle of the fire, reminding me things can always get worse. Then something big and green flashed by me, clipping my skate. I watched Richard Musso pull away and lean into the next pylon like the Tower of Pisa—and knew he had me beat.

Over dinner the night before I'd told my parents about the new injury and my mother had advised me to scratch both my finals to protect my leg. I was coming around to her point of view. I'd torn the same muscles three times, and trying to beat Musso I'd probably do it again. My less admirable reason for backing out was that the guy scared me. His size and power somehow made me feel weak and insignificant. I had an irrational fear he'd humiliate me. When the finalists were called to the starting line, instead of joining them I rolled off the floor and skated up into the bleachers and sat down with my parents to watch the race.

"You're doing the right thing, Bill," my mother said.

Dad said he backed me too, but with less enthusiasm. He'd grown up poor in rural Alabama and had an abiding fear that his sons, raised as well-off city boys, would be weenies. His reaction made me consider how my rink friends were going to view my fade-out. I felt terribly conspicuous sitting with my parents while my race began without me.

Musso won the start and began separating himself from everyone except Rick. Rick stayed with him as he'd stayed with me, drafting on his opponent's greater bulk. I could see now what my wiry friend had been up to in the heats when I'd sensed a storm of activity behind me. After scissoring out of a turn he continued his power strokes up the entire straightaway, in the end dancing sideways in a frenzy. It was his way of keeping pace with a more powerful skater. At the last possible moment he shifted into a glide and swept around the pylon on the leader's heels.

After rounding the final cone Rick challenged on the inside, and he went nuts. My boney friend and Boy Mountain fought it out down to the wire, where Musso won by just enough to make his victory clear. Given their physiques, Rick's performance was more impressive to me than the champion's. My friend's all-out effort to uphold the honor of our rink would have been inspiring had it not made me feel useless and beside the point. I scratched my 440 final and went home to hide out. Sulking in my bedroom, I reviewed bleakly the series of blunders that had dogged me from the start of track season, snuffing out my chances as an athlete. A common thread ran through all of them. I possessed a genius for leaping into action with my head up my ass. Other people did it now and then. It was my default.

I didn't see Katy even once during the weekend of regionals. Our races were scheduled at different times, and also, at age fifteen I hung out mainly with my guy friends while she ran with her sister and their girlfriends. I was glad to hear Katy qualified for nationals again. I was even gladder she didn't see me duck my races. She heard about it from others I'm sure, but never brought it up, just as I never brought up the things I knew embarrassed her. We were pretty good that way.

TWENTY-SIX

D URING the month between regionals and nationals Katy's brother Greg spent an afternoon at our house. He, my brother, Steve Bertholf and I were in the backyard chasing each other around barefoot, playing keep-away I think, when I saw Greg wince in midstride and limp to a stop on the ball of his foot. His uplifted heel was dripping blood fast enough that I knew the cut was bad. Hobbling, he retraced his steps then leaned down and worked out of our lawn the detached steel rim of a one-pound coffee can. He held it up for John and me to see, smiling with the ironic brightness that was his specialty. At first I didn't know what to make of it. Then I remembered knocking coffee cans off a box with a baseball years earlier not far from where Greg stood. If his injury kept him from repeating as national champion it would be my fault.

John went to get Mom while I used the garden hose to wash away the flowing blood so I could see the cut. It spanned the width of Greg's heel and was deep enough that my mother decided it was one for the emergency room. We wrapped the foot in a towel and took Greg to St. Joseph's. Mom phoned Greg's mother from the hospital, thinking she'd want to join us, but on hearing of her son's injury Charlotte went into an emotional tailspin that prevented her driving a car. Later, when we dropped Greg off at his house, Katy said her mom was "resting."

I found Charlotte's response to this relatively minor emergency hard to understand and asked my mother what was going on. Looking bemused and a little sad she said something I've never forgotten. "Bill, most people never grow up." I could see how that applied to Charlotte, but "*most* people"? Did she really mean a majority of adults aren't actually adult? I thought about my friends' parents, and my parents' friends, and my older relatives—who all seemed grown up to me. I asked Mom for examples. Who hadn't grown up? She wouldn't go into specific cases, maybe to protect reputations or maybe because she didn't want to argue, but she wouldn't back off her assertion either. In fact she repeated it. She wasn't being stubborn. She was convinced. Most people never grow up.

As I watched people I knew getting older, I began to see what my mother meant. Most of us don't change in motivation as we age, though we learn more socially acceptable methods to get what we want. All but a few remain fundamentally committed to themselves and to satisfying sometimes infantile desires. Thank goodness for those who do grow up all the way because they provide the colorless glue that binds any social unit composed of humans. The rest of us, toddlers in disguise, merge with our performances so seamlessly that when a mask slips, as during a violent crime, often no one can explain it.

My mother became an adult just by living her life. Born a generation before Charlotte, she transitioned from teen to stand-in parent when her mother was committed to the Kansas state mental hospital at Osawatomie, her home for decades. Mom and her sister Catherine, the two oldest, having little choice in the matter, shared the maternal role. They raised their three younger siblings to adulthood while doing the housework and attending school. Later they supported their parents financially through the Great Depression. Neither made much money (mom was a public school teacher) but they both held steady jobs.

As a mother to me, the Louise Loy who married my dad was as dependable as the sun—and there's only one exception I can think of. Around age nine I was playing King of the Mountain with an older neighbor boy after school. He was standing on a pile of construction dirt swinging a steel pipe over my head as I climbed toward him. He warned me, "Better stop or I'll hit you." Was I going to let him punk me out with threats? I didn't see why. I doubted he had the guts to actually clock me. I took another step up and the swinging pipe smacked me on the side of the head so hard I felt my skull crack. Frightened and seeing stars I ran down the hill and across the street to our house. Once inside I let out a horrific wail and started bawling my head off.

Mom took me into the bathroom and examined my latest wound in the good light there. Her calm voice and careful hands helped me realize I wasn't dead, or even dying, and I relaxed enough to knock off the caterwauling. With my fingertips I felt the bump swelling above my ear. I was sure my mother saw it. She did, but she said it didn't need a doctor. I told her how it happened, thinking she'd want to talk to the boy who piped me or tell his parents—but no. She applied a little maternal medicine by kissing the bump and sent me on my way. I was left wondering why she dropped the matter.

Another time, when I was eleven, I was playing kick the can with some neighborhood teens who'd made me their mascot. One of them booted the can into my forehead, opening a cut that needed stiches. I knew he did it on purpose. I saw his eyes. He was pissed off at me for nearly beating him back to the can. My mother's take on it: "Bill, maybe you shouldn't play with boys so much older. You have friends your age." Similar sequences of events kept happening until I got the message. I was on my own with other guys. Knowing that, I learned to take care of myself, a necessary lesson for someone reluctant to back down.

My mom's most winning feature was her fun side—infectious, zany, always original. It was one reason people of all ages usually took to her. She was a gifted mimic with a wide range of amusing voices and a mobile face that matched each voice with exactly the right look. When she read us the Pooh Bear stories, the cast of Milne's characters came alive in our living room, holding John and me mesmerized the way early television would a few years later. Our marked interest in literature and writing probably began with Mom animating stories for us when we were highly impressionable.

My mother's most glaring weakness? Me. I say that because I think she loved me too much—and a little more than my brother. She did her best to contain her favoritism, but it came out in the way she hugged us, straightened our hair, talked to us. In a restaurant she'd call our family's attention to a very heavy person seated several tables away and say sadly, "Oh, why did he let *that* happen?" In my family only my brother was overweight. Mom may have believed she was nudging her younger son toward a healthier future, but I felt a cruelty in her words very unlike her. I wondered if these comments hurt John, though he never showed it. Maybe he thought they didn't apply to him. Or maybe they hurt so much he couldn't afford to show it.

My brother never had the long, involved talks with our mother that I enjoyed, so he missed a lot of her wisdom. I don't think she taught him how to box dance as she did me. But maybe he didn't want her to. John was more attached to our father, who I believe favored him over me. There was a certain fairness in this, a balancing of imbalances—and it was natural, a matter of similar personalities seeking out their kind for the stronger bond. Mom and I were volatile, my father and John cool headed and somewhat phlegmatic.

My father's experiences in hard times closely paralleled my mother's. When his family's farm and small sawmill went bankrupt in the recession following World War I, he took it on himself to become the main breadwinner. Around age eighteen he left his Alabama homestead to get a good education, then a job that paid enough to provide for six younger siblings and his widowed mother. Land where they lived fell in value to two dollars an acre in the 1930s and some people starved, but not in Dad's family. Their main provider was making good money in Wichita working for the Farm Credit Administration, one of FDR's rural recovery programs, and he sent much of his salary home. Both my parents were proud of their sacrifices for their families, believing I think that this went a long way in defining them as people.

In rural Alabama in 1910 boys didn't play the sports I played. I learned to spiral a football not by tossing one back and forth with my pop but by watching the big kids. By the time I picked up a baseball I'd thrown thousands of rocks, developing accuracy and a novice's heater, so no need for Dad to help me with that either. One sports activity we did share was sprinting. When I was eight or nine my father and I began walking together in the evening to a nearby bakery that sold doughnuts made of potato flour. During our "Spudnut" run one night he challenged me to a footrace in the street. I went for it and we gunned it for forty yards and he beat me. It was fun and I liked knowing that my dad, so much older than the other dads, could probably outrun half of them, maybe most of them. He was really speedy for a fifty-six-year-old desk worker. Our footraces became a regular thing for several years. Then, when I was around eleven, I beat him—convincingly. Wow, I thought, I'm getting fast! I turned to see my father's pride in the son who'd inherited his legs (as well as his name) and learned he was not proud. His face was blank, like he didn't want to admit what had happened. He almost never showed his ego but I saw it that night. We didn't race after that.

Both John and I loved it when our father took us fishing in the woods outside of town. On a Saturday we'd get up at six, grab a quick breakfast, and pick up minnows and night crawlers from a bait shop on Wichita's outskirts. Sometimes we fished a local lake, sometimes a creek. Whichever it was, my brother and I would walk the bank with our spinning gear, fishing every hole, while Dad sat quietly in the same spot for hours holding his cane pole, watching his bobber and thinking.

Given my father's fully developed sense of responsibility he must have been dismayed by my early stumbles while seeking a career path. In 1967, having prepared well to study law, I was persuaded by the tenor of the times and by my own research that I wouldn't like being a lawyer and turned down scholarship offers from Stanford and Duke. A year later I dropped out of a doctoral program in anthropology, having at last determined my adult career: freelance poet and jack of all trades. I was pursuing my chosen profession with gusto when Dad wrote me this letter, which I saved:

Dear Son,

This is a belated reply to your two letters (one written last June and one received several days ago). They are the kind of letters that every thinking parent appreciates because they reflect the gradual unfolding of a maturing young mind.

When Mom and I were married we wanted children more than anything else in the world. We were willing to forgo most anything to be good parents. Perhaps we made our share of mistakes in judgement but not in motive. When we think of you boys today we consider ourselves as very fortunate indeed, and as successful parents.

In the early years we were very strict parents but as you boys

approached 10 or 12 we became less so. By that time it was evi-
dent that you were capable of making some decisions on your
own and of being responsible for any mistakes. We felt that the
errors in judgment made while still with us need not be repeated
when you got out "on your own"....

You have a good heritage, genetically, and have made a good
start in shaping your life in this very fluid society. To establish
goals for one's life and stick to them is not easy in this modern
world. However, without a sense of mission, adjustment to life
would be even more difficult.

We know that both you and John have had a problem in
finding your field of work and deciding the direction your lives
should take. We are happy that both of you are facing the issue
head on now, rather than later. You have made progress the last
year or so and we are confident you will work things out in your
own way—the way that is "right" for you.

Love, Dad

I don't want to give the impression that my parents' marriage
was perfect. As in most marriages, there were strains, well-con-
cealed from my brother and me while we were growing up. We
didn't learn of them until the evening of Father's funeral, as
Mom, John and I kicked back in the family rec room after a long,
emotional day. My brother opened a forty-ouncer and poured
glasses of beer for himself and me. I knew Mother was a teeto-
taler, because she and Dad had always been, but just to be inclu-
sive I asked her if she'd like a glass.

"*Yes!*" she said, leaving no doubt.

That really surprised me. "I thought you didn't drink."

"I did before I met your father. He said it set a bad example for
you boys. But I love beer." She told about the summer parties her
father threw in their backyard as she was growing up. "He would

buy a keg and ice it down till it was really cold. Oh that beer was good! I can taste it now."

Later in the evening she told us that she and Dad had often gone dancing before World War Two. They stopped because he thought dancing was disrespectful while our servicemen were dying overseas. I realized then why my mother had insisted on wearing her bright red overcoat to the funeral instead of her dark grey one. I'd attributed it to her recently diagnosed early dementia, but I think she was making a statement too.

My dad even as a young man was a bit of a stick-in-the-mud, while Mom had been a 1920s flapper with bobbed hair, big brown eyes, and an attitude. I like to look at pictures of her from those years when she was young and showing her pizazz. By the time she married Dad she was in her early forties and I believe was becoming more anxious. My father's extreme stability must have anchored her. I'm sure of this: my parents agreed on what they considered important, from how to live one's life to how to raise a child. I never doubted they belonged together. I like to picture them as I often saw them—sitting side by side, talking, sometimes smiling like a pair of hundred-watt bulbs plugged into the same juice.

TWENTY-SEVEN

DURING the first year Katy and I were together her mother changed boyfriends twice, I believe. The second reshuffling occurred midsummer when Charlotte hitched her star to a larger-than-life West Texas oilman and multimillionaire, E. J. Rafferty. I met EJ at a party for the speed club members and their families paid for by the Texan and hosted by Rick Shafer's dad in the Shafer backyard. When my family arrived Mr. Shafer was tonging chicken quarters onto his barbeque grill. In the shade of the house adults in lawn chairs sipped drinks and talked, while around the pool a dozen teens and preteens in swimsuits were behaving themselves for the most part. A Coleman ice chest stocked with soft drinks sat on the patio next to another containing cold beer. Waiting in the kitchen for those interested were wine, hard spirits, and mixers.

It was not the sort of get-together my parents were used to and they must have been a little uncomfortable. I doubt they minded the drinking per se, but drinking around children was, to my father at least, inappropriate. They were doing what they usually did in such situations—being more polite than usual and smiling more than ever. Mr. Shafer brought them lawn chairs and set them up in the shade where they soon were visited by their young skater friends.

Excitement was in the air. The party was alive with the news that EJ had offered jobs to several guys on the club who were either unemployed or looking to triple their pay. The tycoon needed oilfield workers for his drilling operations and was hiring anyone eighteen or over who asked him for a job. Gloria's Luke had been handed the plum, a gig as oilfield foreman at a handsome salary. Luke was happy and proud, though also a little subdued, like he couldn't quite believe his good luck. His new job probably meant he and Gloria could get married and buy a house—after she finished high school of course. EJ told rest of his new hires they'd have to start at the bottom, doing dangerous and dirty work as roustabouts, but added they'd have the opportunity to learn oil-field production from the ground up, preparing themselves for executive positions later, should they so aspire. On that bright summer afternoon you knew by people's faces there were some high aspirations.

EJ and Charlotte sat centrally located in lawn chairs while several new oil-field workers schmoozed with the boss and hustled to replenish his drinks and those of his first lady. Our cool James Deans had dropped their nonchalance and were exposing their deep desire to make it in life. Obviously they dreamed of jobs that paid enough for them to join the middle class, even if the work was hard and required a move to Texas. They'd no doubt learned that a high-school diploma is no sure ticket to financial security. Lucrative employment by EJ, coming more or less out of thin air, must have seemed manna from heaven.

I wasn't sure I liked EJ but I took him to be what he said he was. Certainly I felt the force of his blunt charisma. He looked really slick in his tooled Western boots, beltless summer slacks and white polo shirt open at the throat, exposing a tuft of grizzled chest hair. His voice was deep and resonant and he spoke in a manner that suggested many people were listening. This two-fisted megabucks was somehow also a man of the people, everybody's buddy. Charlotte sat next to him smiling and riding her personal cloud nine, legs crossed at the ankle, a flattering wide-brimmed straw hat shading her fair face and shoulders. She really did look nice that day. She also looked like someone who had finally assumed her rightful station in life. She laughed a lot and I think she was drinking more than usual. Who could blame her for a little celebration?

I wondered where Katy was. She'd been with us when her mother introduced EJ to my parents but I hadn't seen her since. She wasn't in the pool or on the lawn and I doubted she was waiting in line in the garage to put the hurt on Rick's punching dummy. That left the house. I found her in the master bedroom sitting in a plush chair and staring at an old movie on TV. The film was a black and white from the 1940s, one I didn't recognize. Katy looked up at me with eyes that had lost their life and transparency. Her face was blank. She didn't speak, so I didn't speak. I knew better than to talk to her when she was that way.

I pulled a chair up next to her chair and sat down and pretended to watch the movie she was pretending to watch. It was full of night scenes and featured a large multi-trunked tree that in the course of the story the viewer is whisked past several times at high speed in what might be the heaviest foreshadowing in the history of cinema. When at the story's climax a principal character steers his speeding vehicle into the tree and dies in a fiery crash, it comes almost as a relief. A good flick for watching without really watching.

I thought I knew what was bothering Katy. She hated her mother drinking too much and acting big in front of everybody—especially my parents. Charlotte was having the day she'd dreamed of all her life and Katy knew it would be impossible to dial her down. Not until years later did I think about what my girlfriend must have been going through with EJ as her instant father figure. I stayed with her in the zone of silence as the movie rambled on. I didn't want to leave her alone and I think she appreciated me being there. Anyway, she didn't tell me to buzz off.

A week or so later I learned from Rick that EJ had skipped town, leaving behind a lot of debts, including a rubber check he'd written Rick's dad to cover the party expenses. The oilman had been a phony all along, and of course the jobs he'd handed out so liberally were equally bogus. His oil-field crew, recently happy and hopeful, returned to nonchalance, pretending nothing had happened. I imagine they were used to disappointment, maybe even expected it, but that didn't mean they deserved it. EJ's job promises were cruel and uncalled for, the product of a man's sick need to make a big impression at whatever cost to others.

Months later, in the fall, my father mentioned he'd marked something in the newspaper he thought I'd want to see. It was a short piece on a back page of the main section. The dateline was a town in eastern Colorado and the gist of the report was that a man with multiple aliases, one of them Edward James Rafferty, had been pursued by the Colorado Highway Patrol to a rail crossing where he was forced to stop by a passing freight train. Before the officers could apprehend the suspect, who had a long record of confidence scams and was wanted in multiple jurisdictions, he pulled a handgun from his glovebox and ended his life.

I knew Katy wouldn't want to talk about EJ's suicide with me so I never brought it up. I assumed she and her mother knew about it, though they may not have. Either way, the Texan—if he was a Texan—was out of their lives for good.

TWENTY-EIGHT

I N July 1960, skaters from the Alaskan traveled 450 miles southeast through Yankee territory and into Dixie for the RSROA national speed skating championships in Little Rock, Arkansas. Our club members went alone or with their families in sedans, station wagons, a hotrod or two, and a new Impala convertible. Although my brother and I hadn't qualified for nationals we'd heard enough about them to make us curious—and we liked trips. We found a ride with Terry Pennick and his parents then talked our parents into letting us go and paying our way. Terry was a year older than me and would be racing in the age division above mine.

On a Thursday afternoon Terry's mom drove her son and John and me down to Boeing where we met Terry's dad as his shift ended. Mr. Pennick stowed his lunchbox in the trunk and slid behind the wheel. He continued south into Oklahoma, then angled southeast as night fell and sandwiches began coming out of the Pennick picnic basket. In the wee hours of the morning we rolled into a dark and sleeping hamlet in eastern Oklahoma and sought out the only house in town with its lights on. There we made our first stop of the trip other than a gas station. At that ungodly hour two Pennick relatives served us a hot meal.

Afterward we all sat around on overstuffed furniture as the adults sipped coffee and talked and we boys listened—or not. I remember being very sleepy, and I think I dozed off. Then it was back to the car with Mrs. Pennick taking the next leg.

Not long after sunup we crested a hill and in the valley below I saw a big river that turned out to be the Arkansas. It had come down from Wichita by a different route to cross paths with us. We descended through its flood plain and passed over the brown swirling current which had tripled in width since Kansas. Then uphill to Fort Smith, where we ate breakfast at the home of more Pennick relatives. Terry's father took the last leg. We arrived in Little Rock early Friday afternoon, found our hotel and checked in.

To the best of my knowledge, our whole speed club stayed at the Capital Hotel, built in 1872, a large stone edifice on a bluff overlooking the Arkansas River and Little Rock's old port. The state capitol building and downtown Little Rock were just south of us, within walking distance. Over the years that hotel has hosted a number of US presidents and remains a tribute to the grand nineteenth-century style—with marble staircases, gleaming wood and brass appointments, and hundreds of rooms opening onto long, extra wide hallways. I remember a big ballroom, a formal dining room, a lounge with a dance floor, and on one basement level a fat cat's mini mall. We'd been booked by the Alaskan management into one of the finest hotels in Arkansas and at reasonable rates. Most skaters shared rooms set up for joint occupancy. The room John and I stayed in with two older guys from East Saint Louis, Illinois, contained four single beds arranged in parallel down room center. The bathroom had several sinks and a three-man shower. The room charge, split four ways, was affordable for even the least flush among us.

Male racers from many clubs stayed on our corridor. The female racers were scattered around the hotel, probably to keep us guys from finding them easily. In our male wing there was a lot of socializing inside the rooms and out in the hallway too. Some rooms had an open door policy allowing people to wander in and out freely. I met a speed skater from Detroit who Rick Shafer told me was expected to win our age division. He was an easy-going, friendly guy, and we hit it off. When I learned he ran track at school, I couldn't resist talking him into a footrace in our long hallway. It was a month after regionals and my groin pull was still mending but I thought I could beat him without pushing myself. Soon we were flying shoulder to shoulder past forty yards of closed doors, hoping nobody stepped out in front of us. I won but I didn't learn what I really wanted to know—whether I could have beaten him on skates. I'm pretty sure I'd have won the start but beyond that I can't say. He was a master of the oval, as I later witnessed.

Richard Musso, my nemesis at regionals, didn't make it to Little Rock. Maybe his family couldn't afford to send him or maybe no one else on his Pueblo, Colorado speed club qualified and he didn't want to come alone. Anyway he wasn't there. I didn't especially like the guy, but I knew that in a fairer world he'd have come instead of me. He'd qualified for the championships while I was there because my parents were indulgent and could cover the tab.

Late in the afternoon my brother and I explored the hotel together, something we did often while traveling with the folks. Our two-pack gave us more chutzpah than either of us possessed alone, encouraging us to be as nosey as house detectives. We were casing the subterranean mini mall when we ran into Danny Swafford exiting the barbershop while rubbing his chin to call attention to its fresh and rosy glow. He'd just gotten his peach fuzz and five adult hairs scraped off his face with a straight razor and was feeling like a duke. "It's for Katy," he explained to me. "So I don't whisker burn her tender thighs."

I punched his shoulder almost as hard as I could. "Whisker burn that!"

He grinned at me.

The next morning Katy and I sat on a couch at the end of her hallway looking through movie ads in a newspaper. A theater a few blocks away was showing "Pollyanna," a Disney production with Hayley Mills in the lead. Hayley was playing a girl our age and I thought the film might be worth seeing. After lunch Katy and I walked to the theater in the heat of the early afternoon and, due to my miscalculation, arrived half an hour early. I didn't want to spoil the movie by viewing the ending first, but I did want to cool off, so I steered us into a clothing shop with air conditioning across the street from the theater. My plan was to kill time by pretending to shop for twenty minutes, but the salesman who attached himself to me had plans of his own and I ended up blowing a good chunk of my trip spending money on a pair of ugly chartreuse slacks that made my butt look big.

I have no memory of the movie other than being shaken by Hayley Mills and her classy British accent. What a cutie! I must have had stars in my eyes as Katy and I departed the theater into a blistering Arkansas summer afternoon. I took the opportunity to unkindly reevaluate my girlfriend's looks in the merciless blaze, and my new readings troubled me. Her blue cotton blouse and plaid Bermudas were so much less flattering than Hayley's film wardrobe, her squinting eyes so small compared to Hayley's big round ones, and her humidity-withered ponytail so low on chic when stacked up against the star's professionally styled curls that for the first time since she became my girlfriend Katy didn't seem pretty enough, and I didn't feel like the luckiest guy I knew. I can't say what showed on my face other than peevishness but Katy read it well and liked it not. Walking back to the hotel we had a spat and arrived overheated, out of sorts, and with one of us head over heels in love with Hayley Mills.

Late in the afternoon, not really reconciled after our squab-
ble, Katy and I kept our date to ride to the sports complex with
Christine Moore and her father in his new convertible. Christine's
tall, blond good looks came rather obviously at least in part from
her dad, who was probably the youngest-minded father at the
rink. In his colorful, stylish shirt with its short sleeves turned
up twice and a silver chain bracelet hanging from his tan wrist,
he might have passed for an older speed skater. He was raising
Christine by himself, after a divorce I believe, and from what I
could see their relationship was loving and respectful on both
sides. If there was a happier or more confident teen at the rink
than her, I don't know who it was.

In the hotel parking lot, with the sun low in the sky, Mr. M.
lowered his car's canvas top into its well. We all climbed in and
began an unhurried panoramic tour of central Little Rock as
shadows recaptured the streets at the end of a withering Southern
day. Katy was no doubt keyed up by the races ahead of her and
I should have been helping her relax, but I was bent inward on
myself and not in the helping mood. As I watched the city go by
I wondered why the hell I'd thought coming to nationals was a
good idea. Now I was going to have to watch what I should have
been part of. And who could I blame but myself? At regionals, if
I hadn't been so focused on beating Musso, I could have toned
down my start to protect my injury as I took second or even third
in my division. That way I might have competed for a national
title in Little Rock. My mood was dark as we stepped from the
Impala onto the sweltering asphalt of the sports complex parking
lot and Christine's dad ran up the top on his ride.

Inside the air-conditioned complex Katy and Christine went
to change into their racing threads while Mr. Moore entered the
auditorium carrying a professional-looking camera. I walked
around the crowded exterior hallway with nothing to do except
feel out of place and in the way. This was not at all how it should

have been. Disappointed in myself and annoyed by the crowd, I escaped into the auditorium where I found a seat low in the bleachers at one end of the portable skating floor. The elevated oval was about two-thirds the size of ours back home and had a railing. Older guys from many clubs were warming up. They circled the pylons fast, kicking up powder on the turns and making the hollow wooden risers under the track roar.

Over the PA came a call for the Senior Men's five mile, the longest race in our sport, and the competitors on the oval slowed down and rolled to the starting line. An official with a clipboard arranged them in rows, one behind the other as at the start of a marathon. Two of my teammates in black and gold were in the front row. One of them was Dick Edwards, the reigning Senior Men's national champion. Dick was our team role model and the closest we had to a superhero. He was a twenty-one year old a few inches under medium height with a crewcut, thoughtful light-brown eyes, a hawk nose, wide shoulders, and a superbly conditioned body weighing about 140.

Our hero's start surprised me by being quite unheroic. I lost sight of him in the surge of bodies then saw him coming around the first pylon tied for about sixth with a guy who was inside of him. That guy nudged Dick wide at the second pylon and when my teammate rejoined the line of skaters he was tenth or so, a quarter lap behind the leaders who were flying like bats out of hell. I thought Dick had already lost the race.

I had a lot to learn. Dick quickly caught up with the man in front of him by using the same frenetic scissoring at the ends of the straightaways I'd seen Rick Shafer use at regionals. Dick dogged the guy, drafting on him, breathing down his neck for several rounds of the oval until his challenge became boring to watch. When my attention wandered, an explosion of arms and legs drew my eyes back to Dick gunning it up a straightaway as he passed his opponent on the inside. That skater managed to stay close for a lap, then dropped back as Dick closed in on the next competitor leading him. He shadowed that guy for a while, then passed again. He caught and passed all of those ahead of him until, two miles into the race, he slipped into first.

Dick powered out of the turn in front of me again and again, tireless as a machine, his face taut with strain and determination. He drew air through a small aperture in his pursed lips and his breathing was surprisingly slow. The gritty brilliance of his performance was so awesome I felt queasy. Eventually I couldn't watch. I was beginning to sense I'd probably never be able to do what he was doing. I was like the bigger guys who'd trounced him on the start only to get passed later. I was a sprinter, with little talent for distance races and not much interest in them either. Somewhere within me the bad news was dawning that as I aged and my races got longer, winning would become harder. I couldn't really confront it yet because in my mind I was still geared to becoming our team's next superhero, after Dick retired that is.

Rick Shafer joined me in the bleachers wearing his uniform and skates. He asked me to attach his meet number to the back of his jersey and dropped four little safety pins into my palm. It occurred to me that if I hadn't fucked up he'd be pinning on my number in return. Not a happy thought! After the last stragglers in the Senior Men's five mile exited the oval, Rick's heat took the floor and began warming up and he left to join them. To his departing back I shouted an envious "Good luck!"

Among Rick's competition was my friend from Detroit, skating relaxed and confident, his warm smile dialed down to a glimmer. His flawless style was impressive, as streamlined as his slicked back hair—so smooth he seemed to be ice skating. His speed was deceptive. He was passing guys easily who were working much harder than he was. I could see that if he ever got ahead of me in a race he'd very probably kick my butt. Later I learned he won the Junior Men's national title, as predicted.

Rick's race was still happening when I noticed Dick Edwards standing on the auditorium floor next to the oval while a male skater from another club tried talking him to death. All Dick could do was nod. After that guy left, Katy took his place and began her animated congratulations. It wasn't wrong for her to support her teammate of course. But did she really need to be so chummy about it? She wasn't flirting exactly. She and Dick were bonding as teammates and the bond was a close, affectionate one reserved for insiders. It made me feel very lonely. Dick smiled at my girlfriend then, a smile I had trouble interpreting, and a terrible fear gripped me. Katy's sister had a thing for older guys. Maybe Katy did too.

Dick noticed me watching them and briefly held my eyes. It was like I'd been caught spying. When he offered no sign of recognition and turned back to my girlfriend, I wondered what he was thinking. Then Katy looked up at me. I assumed Dick had told her I was snooping and, although I didn't yet know what a voyeur was, I felt like one. My humiliation fueled an anger tempered not at all by my suspicion I might be way off base.

Eventually the mutual admiration society adjourned and skated away in different directions. I followed Katy. She was moving swiftly on skates and I was in shoes so I had to run. In the exterior hallway clogged with milling people I got close enough to call her name and she stopped and turned toward me. As I approached I could see she knew what was coming. The same thing that came every time I blew a fuse. Blinded by hurt and frustration I handed back her name bracelet and wished her all the happiness in the world.

"I'll give yours back later," she said. "It's in my skate case." With a look of disdain she pushed off.

Knowing my performance required a fitting exit, I marched

to the nearest exterior door and slammed both palms into its horizontal bar, punching through to a humid Arkansas dusk. The door pulled shut behind me and auto locked as I realized I'd launched myself without a plan. I still had my ticket stub so I might have taken a few minutes to regroup before reentering by the main door, but that would have been too sensible, too out of keeping with my volcanic mood. Going with that mood I decided to get even with the world by walking back to our hotel, five or six miles away by my estimate. Wouldn't *that* show Katy who she was dealing with? And what downside could there be? I'd hiked ten miles with the Boy Scouts several times without a problem. I couldn't get lost because I'd paid attention to our route during the drive and was sure I could retrace it. True, there was a chance I'd be maimed or murdered during my long hike through an unfamiliar city on a steamy Saturday night, but that held a certain allure. I relished the thought of Katy wracked by grief and guilt on learning of my demise.

We'd arrived on a wide boulevard that bounded the complex grounds to the north so I began walking back along that. Since there wasn't a sidewalk, I trudged the roadside through mowed grass. The headlights of the cars behind me lit my way more or less, but their illumination wasn't constant and the ground under the grass was uneven, so I kept stepping into hidden depressions. When I got tired of jarring my teeth, I crossed to the other side of the street where sidewalk did exist. The headlights approached me now, blinding me like a deer, and I soon saw that wouldn't work either. Arriving at a cross street I took it north a block, then turned east again down a lightly trafficked avenue between apartment houses and businesses closed for the night.

That street had sidewalks on both sides and good lighting and I followed it many blocks while the businesses and apartments became fewer then disappeared altogether. The new neighborhood was middle-class residential, mostly older homes. I continued on for another mile and was beginning to feel quite friendly toward that loyal street when it dead-ended on a busy two-lane running north and south. I walked north another block then turned east again, secure in knowing I was now exactly two blocks from the boulevard that marked my route.

As I proceeded, the houses became smaller and older and the streetlights dimmer. Then the sidewalk ended in an overgrown front yard. I moved my act to the street, full of potholes and littered with loose surfacing. It was a neighborhood the city government seemed to have forgotten. The cars that passed me now all contained people who were black and I realized I'd wandered into their neighborhood. I was still at least two miles from our hotel and my desire for a violent death had entirely dissipated.

Three years earlier, in 1957, Little Rock had been in the news every night for a couple of weeks when its Central High School was ordered by the US Supreme Court to accept its first black students. On television I watched those nine brave kids, more girls than guys, walk through white yahoos who cursed them, spat at them, threatened to kill them. Given that history, it was easy to imagine that some black people in Little Rock might bear a grudge. I believed in the racial justice those students represented and would have gladly welcomed them to my school, but black people couldn't know that just by looking at me. Naturally, I was afraid. Yet I passed through that neighborhood for many blocks and no one paid me much mind except for three boys around my age standing in a dirt yard at the top of a hill. As I passed they gave me some lip.

"Hey, fool, know where you at?"

"Lookin' for trouble, boy?"

Sensing it wasn't the right time to voice my political and racial views so we could all become friends, I ran down the other side of the hill and away from them—showing respect even as I moved my body toward greater safety. When I was almost out of range, three rocks skipped by me harmlessly on the street. Those guys didn't want to hurt me. They were the young Robin Hood band of their neighborhood, chasing off a suspicious intruder in the night.

The top of the next hill offered a long view south, informing me I'd somehow lost track of the well-lit boulevard guiding my return. I couldn't see it anywhere. Fear was seeping into me when I realized I didn't need any particular street to orient me because every street sign provided the cardinal directions. All I had to do was let the signs direct me east to Spring Street, where the movie theater was located, and Spring would take me north to the hotel.

When I began skirting downtown I knew I was on the right track and relaxed enough to consider a problem I'd been trying to ignore. Inside my penny loafers pain was urgently telegraphing the high probability of blisters. Should I stop under a streetlight and check on the situation? I decided against it, thinking the damage was done, and besides, blisters or no blisters, I had to keep going. Maybe the pain would help toughen me up.

Not long afterward, under a tree limb half a block away I saw a well-lit sign for Spring Street and figured I'd made it. Finding my way back was the only thing I'd done right all day and I began feeling better about myself. Ten minutes later I limped into the hotel lobby, which seemed eerily normal. Upstairs I was surprised to find no one in the hallway or in our room. Then I remembered the banquet.

I slipped off my loafers, uncovering two white crew socks with gruesome toes. Peeling the socks away from the wounds they were stuck to hurt like hell. On top of nearly every toe a broken blister was oozing blood and on the bottom of each heel a large pad filled with liquid floated a bubble. In the shower I washed off five miles of summer sweat then gingerly cleansed my toes. The soap burned in the wounds—disinfecting them, I told myself. I patted the sores dry with what soon became a bloody towel. I pulled on two layers of dress socks to cushion the raw flesh, put on my loafers and limped from the room.

My long hike had burned off my foul mood and given me time to reflect on my embarrassing behavior. Katy had a perfect right to congratulate Dick, even if it made me jealous, and when I broke up with her and left the sports complex instead of staying to cheer her on, I'd been a self-centered ass. It crossed my mind that Mr. Moore and the girls might have searched the complex looking for me before they left, but I realized how unlikely that was. I'd shown them I definitely wasn't worth the trouble.

Limping down the staircase into the ballroom, I saw Katy with members of our club next to a long table where there'd been a dinner. She was wearing the white dress she'd worn to the hospital to visit my mother and her hair was down. She was really looking her best. I approached her with uncertainty, unsure how she felt. I thought she might freeze me out.

"Can we talk?" I asked.

Two or three floors above, at the end of a long hall, we sat on a couch and I tried to explain myself. "Katy, I lost it today. I was an idiot."

She nodded, looking wary.

"I wasn't really mad at you."

"Sure acted like it."

"I was mad at myself—for screwing up nationals. I don't know why I took it out on you."

"There's nothing between Dick and me. We're teammates, that's all."

"I know. You didn't do anything wrong."

"How did you get back to the hotel?"

"Walked."

She didn't look surprised. She knew what I was like.

I asked how her races went.

"Not so good."

"Picked the perfect time to unload my problems on you, didn't I?"

"It's not your fault. I just lost."

"Maybe my bullshit helped you."

She smiled. "Probably not."

She didn't seem as fed up with me as she had a right to be. I decided to push my luck further.

"Has anyone told you how pretty you look?"

"Yes," she said, smiling brightly to rub it in.

I knew better than to ask her who. It was natural for her to get compliments, and actually I kind of liked it. If she hadn't gotten compliments, I probably would have been disappointed.

Why did I keep fighting with this one-of-a-kind person who had everything I wanted in a girlfriend? Well, I knew one reason why. When I got mad I did things I later regretted. I promised myself I'd never lose my temper again, not with Katy.

To her I said, "I don't always act like it, but I do love you."

"I love you too."

As we kissed, I tasted her tears, and she must have tasted mine.

She looked so nice that night I knew I'd been unfair to her earlier. Hayley Mills at her best was no prettier than Katy dressed up. Probably not as pretty. Katy with her hair down and wearing just a touch of makeup was hard to beat. How could I have forgotten that she was Cinderella?

TWENTY-NINE

I N September of 1960 Katy and I left our middle school behind and began East High as sophomores. That same month or the one after we started traveling with the speed club to dual meets in other cities. I'd guess these competitions were something the rink owners and coaches had planned during regionals at the Alaskan, but however they came about, trips to places we'd never been were a great idea. There's something about spending even a day in an unfamiliar town that can open a young mind to life's possibilities. Some of our club members had rarely been outside of Wichita, and especially for them our meets on the road were an education.

In the Alaskan's parking lot one Saturday morning we climbed from our parents' vehicles with our skates or skate cases and boarded a luxurious tourist bus with plush seats that rose high above our heads. Coach Fite did a roll call, then sat down behind the driver and the bus began to roll. We were bound for a meet in Coffeyville, Kansas, 140 miles southeast of Wichita near the Oklahoma border. Our highly energized crew, revved up by the racing to come, filled about half the seats—chattering, laughing, teasing, and changing places as we swept over rural blacktop past harvested fields. Now and then the bus slowed for a hamlet of white frame houses, a few brick ones, two churches, a grocery, and several dozen streets of trees releasing leaves in the wind.

Around noon our tires crunched into a gravel parking lot and the bus hissed to a stop. Skaters poured out and filed into the rink, which was shaped like a military hanger with an arched steel roof. The building looked too small to contain a roller rink, but its interior was surprisingly spacious and had everything required, including a floor half the size of ours at the Alaskan. As a newly minted Intermediate Man, I would be skating two miles, four times the length of my longest previous race. I realized two miles would be a lot of laps on such a dinky floor and began to wonder what that would be like.

My brother and I ate at the lunch counter then suited up in the men's dressing room. I wanted to get a feel for the oval so I joined those warming up and soon learned the floor was not my friend. Coming out of turns I faced such short straightaways that I'd barely begun to accelerate when I was bearing down on the next pylon. Worse, a steel pipe railing had been installed at stomach level between the oval and the bleachers, adding an element of suspense to our events, since no one knew when the next hapless racer would slide out and get piped in the gut at thirty miles an hour. The danger was aggravated by the turns, powdered in a miserly fashion and too slick for safe racing.

Competing with me in the two mile were several Intermediate Men from the Coffeyville club and several from our club. My groin pull was almost healed and didn't figure to be a problem, especially in such a long race. I won the start, got rolling fast, and as I circled the oval five yards ahead of second I felt good. Things were going my way. All I had to do was hold the lead and I'd win. Then I passed the canvas lap counter for the first time and saw how many laps remained—fifty some—and it made me think. Was I going out too fast? I didn't consciously slow down yet it wasn't long until I could sense somebody close behind me.

Glancing back I saw the large nose and big luminous eyes of Terry Pennick, the older teammate my brother and I had ridden to Little Rock with. He was drafting on me, and judging from what I could see of his face he was smiling. Terry had always been slower than me and I'd come to believe he couldn't beat me. Yet now he was dogging me the same way Dick Edwards had dogged his opponents at nationals.

Fifteen laps into the race I was still leading but I was breathing hard and my lungs were starting to burn. Maybe I *had* gone out too fast. The pace didn't seem to bother Terry, though. He was glued to me, waiting for his chance to pass. Although he had me worried, I refused to be beaten by such a plodding racer who, when he sprinted on skates, flailed his arms like he was fighting off bees. His ungainly style amused me until it surged by me on the left, thrashing the air like a broken windmill. I was the better sprinter and beat him to the next pylon but my speed threw me wide on the lightly powdered turn. As I balanced on the verge of sliding out, Terry passed me easily on the inside and took the lead.

I now drafted on Terry as I thought about him being ahead of me. I really didn't like that and refused to accept it because I was convinced he couldn't beat me. My new plan for winning was to stick with him as he'd stuck with me, making him nervous as he had me, and then, when he lost focus as I had, I'd pass him and retake the lead. The problem with my plan was that while I was making him nervous, my air intake became noisier and more painful until I realized I'd have to slow down just to finish the race. Before I knew it Terry was leading me by five yards. When I tried to take back those yards I found I didn't have enough gas in my tank to do it. Soon Terry was twenty yards ahead.

His machine-like style, humpbacked though it was, reminded me more all the time of Dick Edwards. Terry was built something like Dick, small bodied but with a relatively large chest.

Unlike Dick, Terry had skinny legs, legs one would think lacked power, yet late in the race those skinny legs lapped me. Long after Terry had won and skated off the floor I sucked air into my burning lungs and held off a hard charging Coffeyville skater for second place. I was disappointed in my performance but consoled myself with the thought that I'd found out what it took to win at two miles. I needed to develop better wind.

In the evening, with the excitement of the day behind us, a more subdued speed club climbed back on the bus. Like me, Katy had struggled in her first distance race and lost. We were both a little down, but the nice thing about that was we could better sympathize with each other. Coach Fite called roll again and one man was missing. Then the straggler clambered aboard, the driver gunned the engine, and the twilight scene outside began to shift.

On the trip down, Katy and I had held hands. Going back at night with no one sitting across the aisle from us and high seatbacks concealing us from those behind us and those in front of us too, we found ourselves with a lot of privacy. Not many miles out of Coffeyville, with night fields visible under the stars and shadows washing through the bus, Katy and I began making out. Since it was a three-hour trip, the situation seemed promising.

We more or less repeated what we'd done in the easy chair a year earlier, except that this time when Katy began losing control she came to her senses and moved my hand to a neutral site. Still, we were making progress. The middle buttons of her blouse were undone and her pedal pushers were unzipped and I was exploring inside her clothes. As I was touching her belly through her panties, Katy moved my hand again.

Then she said, "I feel sleepy." I was disappointed that she wanted to sleep rather than make out, but how could I tell her no? I expected her to turn away from me and pull her legs up onto the seat, but instead she turned to face me and moved closer so that our heads came together, placing her body within easy reach. She fell asleep remarkably fast, making me suspicious. I thought she couldn't possibly be in dreamland so soon. And why hadn't she refastened her clothes?

Was her partially undressed availability an invitation? It was so dark on the bus that someone passing in the aisle would have had trouble seeing what I was up to, if I chose to be up to something, and I did. I moved so close to sleeping beauty that my forehead pressed her bangs, then I went back to my gentle explorations, but without the kisses. Although I missed the kisses, and although petting Katy while she pretended to sleep seemed somehow a little seedy, we worked out a game we would play again. She allowed me liberties up to a point slightly beyond the point I'd reached before, and then, without opening her eyes, she moved my hand away from what remained off limits. She "fell asleep" again and the cycle repeated.

Late in the trip I was able to slip my fingers under her bra from the top. When she inhaled, her nipple touched my fingertips, swelling from the contact. I was getting very excited when she collared my wrist and moved my hand again.

Our game continued until we entered the Wichita outskirts on East Kellogg and the bus filled with light and Katy opened her eyes. She refastened her clothes and became her usual self, and I wasn't sure what to think. I'd gotten a pretty good buzz, maybe she had too, but the way we'd done it left me feeling empty. And I was confused. Where had the Katy gone who'd melted down in the easy chair? I missed that girl.

THIRTY

OUR next dual meet was in Topeka, the state capital, 140 miles northeast of Wichita on the route to Kansas City. On a bright Sunday afternoon in October we travelled again by luxury bus, this time on the Kansas Turnpike through the Flint Hills. The Topeka rink was located in a place you'd never guess—high in a building near the heart of downtown, where fortress-like tributes to the nineteenth-century stone mason's art were mirrored in contemporary glass office towers. Our driver parked in front of an architectural grandfather, a ponderous four-story limestone with big dark windows under heavy brow ridges.

Coach Fite led our platoon of thirty up wide stone steps worn swayback by several million feet. We passed through heavy oak doors and ascended a beautifully crafted wooden staircase that creaked and snapped and groaned beneath us, complaining of a century's hard use. We got off on the third or fourth floor and entered a spacious high-ceilinged room containing a skating oval about the size of the one in Coffeyville. It was flanked on one side by permanent wood bleachers and on the other by tall windows. Skating past those windows covered in wire mesh I could look down forty feet onto a city intersection. It was weird speeding on skates so high above the almost empty Sunday evening streets.

In the Intermediate Men's two mile I won the start by force of habit, stretched my lead a bit, then got reeled in and eventually passed by Terry Pennick and later by a guy on the Topeka club. Before the race was over, Terry lapped me twice. I wasn't getting better as an Intermediate it seemed—he was. Not really surprising because in the month since losing in Coffeyville I'd done little to develop better wind. The sport I once loved no longer excited me. I'd stopped being good at it and my athletic ambitions had already shifted to high school track, where I'd be able to compete again as a sprinter.

On the way home we stopped for dinner at the first restaurant south of Topeka on the Kansas Turnpike and our team overwhelmed the servers with counter orders and takeout. Getting our food took time but eventually, with some of us still eating, the bus began to move again. As soon as we were beyond the lights of the rest area Katy and I shared a kiss. This time we had two hours to fool around and much the same thing happened that had happened coming back from Coffeyville. We steamed up the window next to us for an hour, then Katy fell asleep unbuttoned and unzipped and let me pet her. Our high-water mark as lovers was attained that night when I managed to finagle my fingers under the top of her panties and down to the place where I thought I'd find her sweet spot. What I found was the smooth skin of her firm lower belly at the junction of her tightly clamped thighs.

I was wondering where the heck she'd hidden it when my girlfriend's sleeping hand gripped my wide awake one and transferred it to my thigh. Our bus was skirting El Dorado then, so I knew we were only twenty minutes out of Wichita, too little time for another foray. Later I tried to figure out why I'd failed to locate the thing I sought, a biological item I knew Katy must possess. Obviously it was located in a place I hadn't yet searched. Probably it was over the boney cliff I'd touched and down in the valley below. If it wasn't there, she didn't have one.

THIRTY-ONE

OUR longest trip with the speed club that fall was in November, an overnighter to Springfield, Missouri, 250 miles east. Around midnight on a Friday Luke and the three Linseys picked up John and me at our house in Luke's black 1957 Fairlane with gold stripes and Ford Motor Company's most muscular V8. I'd always liked the way Luke drove. He had enough horsepower under his shoe to shut down anything but a Stingray, yet motored with unusual prudence, showing courtesy to other drivers and total obedience to the laws of the road. With his narrow blue eyes locked on the highway ahead he eased us through eastern Kansas on a chilly prairie night. The warm car interior and the rumbling of glass packs made me a little sleepy. An hour out of Wichita, Katy curled up in the middle of the back seat with the top of her head touching my thigh and zonked out for real, sleeping like the dead. My brother, sitting up across the seat from me, fell asleep too. Eventually only Luke and I were awake. I tried to sleep but was too wired by the excitement of being out of town with Katy for two nights and a day. Far from our parents and the usual restrictions, who knew what might happen?

Dawn was overcast. In the muted light I saw we were passing through low mountains covered with hardwoods stripped of leaves. During the night we'd climbed a piedmont into the Ozark Mountains. Surrounding us were a million naked limbs blackened by rain and raised to a lead sky. On slopes under the trees lay their fallen colors, turning brown. Much the same scenery stayed with us as we continued east and one by one the sleepers woke. When everyone was up, Gloria handed out breakfast sandwiches.

On the outskirts of Springfield Luke and Gloria dropped off us younger ones at the roller rink and departed to enjoy the day by themselves. I didn't see them race and doubt there was a race for skaters Luke's age. I realized they'd come to Springfield to spend time alone together. Where they went I'm not sure. I could think of places I might go if Gloria was my girl and we were out of town and she was agreeable. Katy and I were left in charge of our brothers, who knew that if they didn't make trouble for us we'd let them do about anything they wanted.

The rink was just inside the entrance to an old fairground closed for the season. As we walked into the aging, single-story building we were greeted by the smell of musty wood, rosin powder, and grilled hamburgers. The oval was small, like those in Coffeyville and Topeka, and a long row of windows followed one straightaway. We Intermediate Men were competing at two miles again and I wasn't hopeful, having been beaten convincingly at that distance twice.

Sprinting for the first pylon I broke one of the front wheels on my right skate. The wheels I'd broken earlier had all flown to pieces, spilling their ball bearings across the floor, but this wheel broke partially. It dropped a big chunk of wood, remaining otherwise intact. Although I was leading the race, every time I put my right skate to the floor a violent vibration shook my leg, slowing me down and jackhammering every ear in the building. The whole field was bunched up behind me impatient to get around and soon they were passing. I let everyone go by, then rolled off the floor. There was really no point in continuing unless my goal was to give a rink full of people headaches.

Katy lost again too. Probably she was getting used to it, like I was. We weren't really interested in the other races, so we went outside under a gray sky and explored the fairground. Few things are more silent than a closed fairground and it wasn't long until the empty stands and dark, vacant stalls began to spook our teen psyches conditioned by horror flicks. We exited the fairground into the woods beyond.

Everything seemed to be part of a gigantic public park. I'd heard from several people about a cave worth seeing, and following their directions I took us through trees down a gently sloping hill covered in leaves. The day was cool and the smell of decaying vegetation hung pleasantly in the moist air. At the bottom of the hill we ran into the end of a lake that opened out spaciously on our right for as far as I could see. The carpet of leaves on the ground extended onto the lake bottom.

When I turned around I saw the cave about fifty yards uphill from us. It was not impressive—a concrete mouth opening into a passage that led back into the hillside. We climbed to it and found its whitewashed cement dingy with age and covered in graffiti. Really it was more a tunnel than a cave, a tunnel shored with an arched concrete lining. It looked long abandoned, but I thought it might at one time have been a fairground amusement. Katy looked a little apprehensive as we walked inside holding hands. We went as far back as daylight reached. Then, confronted by inscrutable darkness, we stopped.

My girlfriend had by now figured out that my interest in the cave was biological rather than geological. She seemed dubious when I leaned down and found her mouth with mine and she kissed me back without the usual enthusiasm. Hmm, I thought, maybe she needs to get warmed up. I kissed her again and this time it felt like I was putting my lips on a store mannequin. Her lack of passion made me more aware than I had been of the short-comings in the tunnel of love I'd found for us. It was indeed a sad one, strewn with cigarette butts and gum wrappers and tagged with the sentiments of long expired relationships. The place even smelled wrong. I tried to meet Katy's eyes but she wouldn't meet mine. She looked unhappy. We left the cave and walked back to the rink out of tune and not holding hands.

As the meet was wrapping up late in the day, Luke and Gloria returned looking pleased with themselves and the rest of us piled in the car. We departed Springfield with the autumn sun setting in our faces. I remember the scene clearly because a powerful and unsettling mood arose in me. I was away from home with a couple all but married and a girl who might become my wife, and it made me feel grown up, almost on my own. The emotion was bittersweet though. It mixed apprehension over leaving my family with excitement concerning my future as a man—when, like Luke, I'd be able to have full relations with my girlfriend. I dreamed of the future while darkness slowly swallowed us and the horizon receded from the sky to the car interior lit faintly by dash lights. All of us were quiet as Luke's black panther with stripes of gold purred homeward through the night.

THIRTY-TWO

M Y sophomore honors English class was taught by Melvin Semple. He was in his early twenties, average in height and weight, and built in the shape of a bowling pin. His sky-blue eyes regarded our class with apparent confidence from beneath a carelessly tended ultra-blond flattop. He wore what most of our male teachers wore back then but with a personal flair. The shoulders of his suit jacket were much wider than his own shoulders and its sleeves draped over his knuckles. His pants pooled on his shoes. I'd heard through the honors program that he'd recently graduated with distinction from a prestigious university and that big things were expected of him. Was he an unworldly genius of some kind? That could explain the clothes.

He promised that ours would be no ordinary English class. To prove it he touched on several course highlights. The one that sold me was his promise to let us write a short story in place of one of the required papers. For two years I'd been spending most of my spare time reading fiction, and I'd begun thinking about writing a story. Here was my chance.

After Mr. Semple's ten-minute introduction to the course he gave us the rest of the hour for a study period. He slipped off his jacket and hung it over the back of his chair, then sat down at his desk and did paperwork while we read or goofed off. I took the opportunity to study the purple stain that began in the middle of our teacher's lower lip and continued down to the rise of his chin. I'd noticed it earlier (hard not to) and now I saw how it had come about. As he corrected papers he sometimes paused to think, and while thinking he rested the business end of his blue ballpoint between his lips and nursed it. Such a tic was not a positive sign in an educator but I reminded myself he was going to let me write a story.

Mr. Semple's first assignment was for us to research an East High extracurricular activity then make an oral report about it to our class. He mentioned a few possibilities: the chess club, the Latin club, East's drama program, and so on. When the time came to have our choices approved, my hand rose with many others. Maybe because my hand was the most insistent, Mr. Semple called on me.

"East High's track team," I said with pride.

He started to reply, then closed his mouth and looked doubtful. "The track team?"

"Sports are extracurricular activities, right?"

"Well, I suppose, but wouldn't you rather report on the drama program? It's renowned throughout the state."

"Our track team has a national reputation." I wasn't entirely sure that was true but thought it probably was. From the sports section in the newspaper I knew that East's head track coach Bob Timmons had a reputation for developing exceptional runners, most recently Archie San Romani Jr., who two years earlier had set a new national prep record in the mile.

Mr. Semple's face clouded up, but he gave in quickly—realizing I think that he couldn't deny my choice without looking like a stinker. "All right. East High's track team. Who else?" Hands went up again. Our teacher pointed to a tall, thin guy in a colorful striped polo shirt whose hand was waving the most enthusiastically of those that remained. "Yes?"

"East High's golf team."

Having accepted my choice, Mr. Semple was forced to accept this one too, but he did it without comment and with a dead face. After writing it down he announced we now had ample reports slated on sports teams and needed coverage of other stimulating activities available to the East High student. Later I would view this minor faceoff as the point at which my student-teacher relationship with Mr. Semple began to sour.

When the time arrived for our first book report I chose Robert Louis Stevenson's *Treasure Island* from the reading list our teacher gave us because I'd heard from friends it was a good story. I read the book, enjoyed it, and wrote the report carefully, hitting all the points our teacher specified. My paper came back a week later with a B on top, a full grade below what I'd expected. I looked for written comments and found none, although a couple of split infinitives had been corrected. Since I couldn't understand what I'd done wrong, and since I wanted higher grades on the book reports to follow, I asked Mr. Semple after class how I could improve.

"*Treasure Island* isn't a very challenging book for someone your age. I was surprised you chose it."

"It's on our reading list."

"The reading list is for all East High sophomores. But you're in an honors class. You should aim higher. The book you chose is just an adventure tale, basically a children's story."

That stopped me. I hadn't known any better than to read a book meant for kids. His judgment seemed right because I figured most kids would like *Treasure Island*. Having my literary retardation exposed so glaringly by a literature teacher made me feel really stupid.

Mr. Semple was writing on a piece of paper with his blue

ballpoint. He handed me the paper. It read: The Brothers Karamazov, Fyodor Dostoyevsky. I'd heard of the book but when I looked on our reading list it wasn't there, though *Crime and Punishment* by the same author was. *The Brothers Karamazov* seemed to be a special book Mr. Semple had chosen just for me. Maybe he knew I wanted to redeem myself by busting my balls, academically speaking.

After school I stopped by the East High library and looked for a copy of the novel. Only one was waiting in the fiction section, an oversized volume printed in a small typeface with two columns per page. It was a thick book and would be by far the longest book I'd ever read. Good, I thought. I'll be able to show Mr. Semple what a willing drudge I am.

Sitting on our living room couch after dinner I opened *The Brothers Karamazov* on my lap and began to read. The events in the book seemed to be happening in Russia long ago, but before I could get a handle on the story I became confused by the tricky Russian names and smothered by the dialogue, which seemed less like dialogue than minutely articulated philosophical positions. Ten pages in, I was sitting up asleep with the book on my lap and my chin on my chest. Later I woke, read some more, and fell asleep again.

For three or four nights I attempted to penetrate the mysteries of *The Brothers Karamazov* but could never understand what was going on except in a general way. Also, reading the novel continued to affect me like a sleeping pill. I finally decided to give up on a book I thought I wasn't ready for. My parents, who'd been watching me struggle like Sisyphus with his rock, supported my decision. I returned to our approved reading list and found a novel written a century earlier by an Englishman, George Eliot. I knew the book was assigned in high school English classes and didn't see how my teacher could object to it. I read it, liked it well enough, and wrote what to me was a solid report. When that paper received a B+, I decided Bs were probably as good as I could expect from Mr. Semple for my book reports. Fortunately, they didn't count for much of our course grade.

The assignment I'd been waiting for arrived late in the semester. At the time I was averaging a high B in Mr. Semple's class, not far from the A I wanted, but my teacher seemed to have me firmly pigeonholed as a run-of-the-mill honors student. I planned to use my short story to blast him out of his grading rut. I'd been incubating the plot in my head for some time and liked what I had. The action seemed top-notch and it built to that jaw-dropping twist I knew the best stories possess. It was derived in a general way from the short fiction I was reading outside of school—Ray Bradbury, O. Henry, de Maupassant, and story anthologies purporting to be edited by Alfred Hitchcock. I borrowed the general situation from Richard Connell's "The Most Dangerous Game," but I gave Connell's story a new plot and a whiplash snap at the climax so wrenching it almost required a seatbelt.

My protagonist loses consciousness in a San Francisco bar and wakes on a tropical beach with nothing but his clothes, a deer rifle, a clip of cartridges, and a splitting headache. He decides the fire power was provided so he could hunt food, but revises his view when a whining bullet clips his ear and he understands he's in a fight for his life. He and his antagonist stalk each other for two days on the small island they share. The other gunman is expending shells as frugally as he is, suggesting they started with the same number. He's still trying to figure out what's going on while he tracks the now familiar size-thirteen boot prints when a rifle slug smacks into the back of his head, pitching him forward onto the forest floor. He bleeds out through his half-missing face.

The story resolves as the protagonist's killer and several other men gather around the corpse. All are dressed in camouflage. From their conversation we learn they are members of a hunting club with a special interest—pitting themselves individually against another hunter in a contest to the death. The fifty-three hours and some minutes required for the current kill is too long a time to qualify the shooter for the finals of the competition, but he receives a commendation for the accuracy of his kill shot.

Not a great story, I now know, and too dependent on the fiction of another author, but it was a story that worked, revised many times, so the C+ it received hit me hard. A C+ in an honors class is basically a failing grade. Ashamed, I told no one.

That spring Mr. Semple allowed himself to be manipulated by a very bright and occasionally devious student from another of his sophomore English classes. Dan Millis gave up his study hall to volunteer as Mr. Semple's "student assistant." Dan would stroll into our room unbidden in the middle of our teacher's lesson plans and ask with feigned obsequiousness if there were any errands for him to run. Sometimes Mr. Semple had an errand and sometimes he didn't, but either way Dan would find a way to mock him—for example, using two fingers to form horns behind our teacher's head. Some of us would laugh and then Mr. Semple would look a little confused, apparently unsure why we were laughing. Today I think he knew what was going on but was afraid to confront it. By the end of our year together part of me felt sorry for him, and the rest of me wanted to rough him up.

I guess he didn't think too highly of me either because in the fall I discovered I'd been quietly booted off honors English track. I didn't accompany most of my nerd buddies as they passed into the nurturing guidance of the two best literature and writing teachers at East. During my junior and senior years I listened to my more fortunate friends rave about their English nirvanas while, sick with jealousy, I suffered boredom in purgatory. Mr. Semple must have written a very negative evaluation of my work in his class. Maybe he felt it was his duty, because at times he did seem genuinely convinced I was dumb as a stump. Let's just say

I was not the type of sophomore English student he was looking for.

What hurt me most was Mr. Semple's opinion of my short story. At the time I saw his grade as an accurate assessment of my story writing ability. He was the teacher, after all—college educated and well read—me just another high school sophomore with pretensions. I wouldn't write my second story until the summer after I finished college—safely beyond all my English classes.

A few years after our time together I heard Mr. Semple had lost his job at East. The news strengthened my faith in my high school but I again felt sorry for a guy who couldn't seem to get a handle on life. His head was lodged so high in the clouds I couldn't imagine him finding much success outside the academic world. However, if what he needed was to get some sense knocked into him, his firing may have been the right medicine.

THIRTY-THREE

Early in March of 1961, a year after I pulled my groin muscle, my leg was completely healed. With high hopes I filled out a multipage application for East High's track and field team. One of the forms stated a prohibition against competing in a school sport while at the same time pursuing another sport and required me to swear I wouldn't. That was easy. Speed skating as an Intermediate Man had become a drag and I gladly checked the box that committed me to monogamy with track. Then I quit the speed club, though not the Alaskan. The rink was where I saw Katy. She remained on the speed club. High school sports didn't exist for girls in 1961, neither in Kansas nor in most states.

During the opening days of track season rain kept the team indoors. On those dark, blustery afternoons Head Coach Bob Timmons and Field Coach J. D. Edminston trotted us to the school gym where we ran laps, did calisthenics and played basketball on the six hoops. The first practice without rain the coaches took us to the track and under threatening clouds clocked each of us running the hundred. I tied with several others for fastest time. A year earlier my good tryout times had led to a pulled muscle, so this time I geared down my expectations. I allowed myself to believe I'd probably make the team.

The next day it rained off and on. Coach Timmons gave the runners their assignments then took my friend Roger McCune and me to the equipment shed and had each of us grab two high hurdles. Following Coach we lugged the hurdles to the gym while Timmons carried his clipboard and a long steel tape in a canister the size of a Frisbee. The hurdles were the old wooden kind, heavily reinforced to withstand brutal punishment. They were painted white to represent, it always seemed to me, little white fences. Like fences, they were hard to knock over and dangerous to tangle with.

Coach had us put down our load on the basketball court. He then provided some motivation, his specialty. He congratulated us for doing well in the hundred but explained that only juniors and seniors would compete in sprint events at the meets. What he needed, he said, was a sophomore to run high hurdles for the varsity. He offered us the chance to compete for that slot. I regretted having to beat out a friend to make the team, yet it did seem a fair way to choose a hurdler.

With Coach directing us, Roger and I positioned the hurdles ten yards apart down the center of the gym. We took turns going over them while Timmons watched, sometimes commenting. Running those old clunkers on a wood floor was a little scary and I'd guess one thing Coach wanted to see was whether we had the nerve to trust in our athleticism and the Lord. Since Roger and I were more afraid of not making the team than of breaking a bone, we put on a show as our basketball shoes squeaked with authority on the lacquered court.

Each afternoon at the start of practice my teammate and I set up adjacent rows of high hurdles then raced each other repeatedly through 120 yards, the distance of our event. At Roosevelt the year before Roger had been our first-string hurdler, and he'd won the hurdles event at the junior high championships. Without a doubt he was a better hurdler than me. But I was faster on my feet, and a better jumper, which evened things. My long stride meant getting my steps right was never a problem and as my technique improved from lamentable to passable I began winning the races. At first I won by a little and then by more. My friend saw what was coming and ceded me the slot on the team before we ran for coach. Certainly there was no need to feel sorry for Roger. He would letter in two other sports, quarterback our football team as a senior, and win an appointment to the Air Force Academy.

At my first track meet I qualified for the finals of the high hurdles and then in the run for medals took fifth. I was disappointed but got a tutorial on how to execute my event from Southeast's Tippy Dye, a sophomore like me. Dye had enviable foot speed *and* flawless form. When he hurdled, his head floated forward at the same elevation while the rest of him kicked and stretched and contorted over the barriers so fast it was hard to follow what he was doing. I wanted to become as good as him by the end of the season but found that difficult. Though I lowered my best time at each successive meet, each meet was bigger than the one before and the competition stiffer, so my improvement didn't show in the results. I would usually qualify for the finals then finish out of the medals—fourth or fifth or sixth.

We all have heard a million times that sports can teach young people important life lessons. That year in track I learned it can be true. I'd always had an easy time in sports based on my speed and had come to believe I was something special as an athlete. Then my string of defeats in hurdling showed me how *unspecial* I actually was, teaching me humility. One of my teammates drove the lesson home by living out my sprinter dreams right in front of me. Bob Hanson, a physician's son, was a year ahead of me in school. He was my height but fifteen pounds lighter, made of little more than fast-twitch muscle fiber and bone. He was good looking, with regular features and straight dark hair.

He sometimes had a word of encouragement for me, a younger sprinter on his team. I envied him but I liked him too.

Hanson became the best sprinter in the history of our school, rewriting much of the track and field record board fastened high on the wall in the men's gym. He won many state titles in the 100, the 220, the 440, the high hurdles, the low hurdles, and could have won a championship in the long jump too if he hadn't been helping East's sprint relays to their medals. At the end of his senior year, competing against some of the best prep runners in the country, he won the quarter mile at the Golden West Invitational in Los Angeles. Bob's stride was no longer than mine but his turnover was so phenomenal that at top speed his limbs nearly blurred. There was no way I could beat him. His electrical system was superior to mine.

Not surprising that Hanson's exceptional talent flowered at East. Coach Timmons was probably the most effective prep coach in Kansas, as dedicated and focused as they come. He was a five-foot, four-inch World War II Marine veteran with a pot belly, no detectable posterior in the seat of his light-blue cotton slacks, the darkest five o'clock shadow I've ever seen on a human, and a mischievous, rather sweet smile radiating happiness and high spirits. Believing we were all capable of athletic feats beyond what we thought possible, he tried to find the right buttons to push in each of us so we could share his vision. We were very aware of his record of success with those who'd preceded us at East so we trusted him. In some ways he resembled my other fine coach, Bob Fite of the Alaskan Speed Club. Both men were devoted to timing and clipboards and record keeping, maybe because they'd served in the military.

To those on our team able to appreciate such things, Coach Timmons showed what one man can accomplish by working tirelessly at a career he loved. Based on what I saw in gym class and at track practice he must have been on the go from the time he woke until he went to bed—always fully engaged and enthusiastic. He was East's head coach not just in track but also in cross country and swimming, and in those sports too his athletes won state titles and sometimes broke national records.

At any given time, it seemed, Coach Timmons had at least one runner in his track stable as remarkable as Hanson. Usually it was a middle distance runner rather than a sprinter. Before Coach left East to become head track coach at the University of Kansas he trained one of the greatest prep athletes ever, a tall, skinny miler from a working-class family who succumbed completely to the Timmons spell. During my senior year of track I saw the budding of Jim Ryun.

Timmons inspired not just great athletes. A surprising number of fairly average East High track team members later reached the tops of their adult professions, including pediatrician Robert Nickel and my vote for best US Secretary of Defense since World War II, Robert Gates, who brokered peace when others wanted war. Both were on the team with me and I think they modeled themselves at least in part on Coach Timmons as they pursued their careers. Gates has said publicly that he did. Many of us who were coached by Timmons left East High confident we could shape our own destinies with careful planning, hard work and perseverance. We'd seen it done on a grand scale.

THIRTY-FOUR

L ate that spring I invited Katy to join my mother, my brother and me for a picnic at a large rural recreational park owned and operated by a group of Wichita public school teachers. Mom was a charter member. RAFT occupied ten acres in farm country east of town and offered educators and their families a place to kick back. There was a two-story clubhouse containing most board and table games known to fanatics, a lake bounded on two sides by elm woods, and a long picnic area along the lake with tables under trees. On shore two or three unsecured canoes containing paddles awaited anyone interested. There were fish in the lake—crappie, bass and bluegill mostly—and bigger fish in the major creek that served as the property's rear boundary, including catfish weighing half as much as I did. Mom usually took John and me to RAFT so we could work our spinning reels, but on this day there would be no fishing. We were limited to things Katy might like. She did not like to fish.

John rode up front with Mother while Katy and I rode in the back seat, our usual post. I was realizing I probably hadn't made clear enough to my girlfriend the nature of our destination, unintentionally misleading her about how to dress. Ideal for her that day would have been her dependable cotton blouse,

Bermudas, and ponytail. But she'd heard me say RAFT was for "school teachers" and I think she'd decided that more formal clothes were advisable. She'd worn her white party dress with her hair down to her shoulders and glowing in the sun. She looked so nice she might have been on her way to Easter service at her Lutheran church. Katy at fifteen and a half was on the verge of womanhood and strikingly pretty.

When she noticed me staring at her she gave me a quizzical look. I leaned close and spoke in a voice too low for the others to hear. "You're so beautiful it's killing me." I wanted her to know that in case she later felt overdressed. In my eyes she was *perfectly* dressed.

"Thank you." Her smile was lovely but subdued—and I knew I'd said the right thing, for once.

At RAFT we drove past the clubhouse and descended to the lake where we found all the picnic tables occupied. Mom parked at the top of a grassy incline sloping to the water and we unloaded the car. Sitting on a blanket in the shade of an elm we ate lunch from our picnic basket. My mother always found ways to make family outings a little special, and on this day she'd trimmed the crusts off the sandwiches and fixed a carton of deviled eggs. For dessert, her dark chocolate fudge.

On a previous visit I'd come across a place I wanted to show Katy. I told Mom we were going for a walk then led Katy through the picnic area and into the woods. We followed a footpath through the trees and eventually arrived at a small grassy open space on the rear boundary of the property. Hydrangea bushes were in bloom, scenting the air. Down a steep embankment the silty water of Four-Mile Creek flowed just perceptibly. Birdsong punctuated the quiet and a picnic table with built-in benches offered a place to sit. To me this leafy glen seemed in every way the antithesis of that smelly cave in Missouri—providing just the atmosphere for romance.

Katy's cologne and radiant whiteness in the heart of green nature were erotic. So was her beauty. When I kissed her, she kissed back willingly, and I sensed the afternoon going my way. Several kisses later, as I smelled her body warm from the sun and saw the top of her bra down her scoop, I moved my hand from her waist to her ribs. During our next kiss I lifted my thumb and gently pressed the underside of her bra through her dress. She let me do it for a while then came out of our embrace. "Maybe we should go back," she said, "before your mom gets worried."

Her shift in mood felt to me like rejection. I said sarcastically, "Worried about what? Bears?" When she didn't respond, I forgot romance and, disappointed, walked with her back to the others.

Even at the time I knew I wasn't being fair. Katy was always on her best behavior around my mother and her best behavior surely included keeping her clothes on during a family picnic. What bothered me was that my girlfriend's retreat from engagement was just the latest in a series of similar withdrawals. We seemed to be moving backward in our physical relationship and I couldn't understand why. My knowledge of such things was composed mostly of hearsay, but the information I'd amassed over the years had led me to expect *forward* progress.

Today I know we needed to talk. We needed to figure out, together, a way around our impasse. Unfortunately, like most teens of our generation we didn't know how to talk, not to each other, especially not about sex, and the problems confronting us were too complicated to resolve by reading each other's eyes. I think if Katy had been able to tell me that her friend Lindy's pregnancy had made her cautious, or that she was afraid of growing up to be like her mom, I'd have understood her reluctance to be the amorous girl of my fantasies. But would I have been mature enough to stop putting the moves on her without being resentful? That I don't know. Loving her when she was passionate seemed to be what I wanted most.

THIRTY-FIVE

RAFT was also the scene of an incident involving the other main woman in my life, the one who shared the longer history with me. My mother and I were always close, and we must have been especially close in the years before my brother came along. John's birth three years after mine was difficult for me and the earliest photos of us together attest to this. I look like I'm waking up after a really bad drunk. The trauma of having to share my mother apparently hit me hard. John in the same photos beams toothlessly like the carefree infant he was, not a thought in his cranium beyond the nipple. But of course he'd never experienced the undivided measure of our mother's love. He never knew what I lost.

During my teen years my tight bond with Mom virtually guaranteed friction between us as I broke away from both parents to become my own man, so to speak. I would often feel mothered to death and it rankled like ice water down my back. I responded by driving her off with sarcasm and mockery, which I could see hurt her. Hurting her made me feel guilty but not guilty enough to tone down my hyper prickly insistence on being left alone. Sometimes my mother was right to intervene in my affairs and sometimes she was wrong, but even when she was wrong her involvement stemmed from her concern for my wellbeing. Often it was simply that she didn't want her headstrong older son to land up in the emergency room again with something else to stitch, X-ray, or pump.

On the day I have in mind Mom had driven John and me to RAFT so we could fish and I'd gone off by myself and was standing on the road that crossed Four Mile Creek with my line in the water. The dam beneath the road held back a big pool where bass and crappie liked to congregate. I could hear water trickling through the overflow pipes beneath me as I watched my bobber vibrating and moving away at a crawl. The activity told me my minnow was alive and kicking against its fate, a good thing by the cruel logic of fishing because the desperation of the little baitfish improved its function as a lure.

I heard someone descending the road from the picnic area and saw it was Mom negotiating the slope in her medium-heeled orthopedic shoes that she wished were more stylish. She was trying not to make noise because she knew it could scare away the fish. She walked across the concrete bridge to where I was standing. "Having any luck?" she asked.

I shook my head no. My bobber had become still. When it remained still I decided that either the minnow had died or a crawdad had snatched it. I reeled in my line and lifted the bait out of the water, then swing it up to me. The minnow was limp in my hand and already losing color. I took it off the hook and tossed it behind me on the bridge for a bird to find. Stepping to the edge of the bridge, I squatted and began lifting the bait bucket out of the water by its nylon cord.

"Bill, be careful," my mother said.

"I am being careful."

"You're so close to the edge."

Seeing no reason to be afraid of a five-foot fall into water, I said, "If only Captain Ahab's mother had watched over him."

Mom knew not to say more. She waited behind me while I opened the bait bucket, scooped up a handful of minnows and released them until I held just one, the one that felt like it had the most fight. I pushed the hook in behind its dorsal fin as it beat its tail against my fingers. Then I picked up my rod and raised it overhead. Swinging the bobber and bait behind me I began to cast.

"Bill, don't...!" Mom cried softly. I knew from her tone that something was very wrong. Turning, I saw my hook caught high in her cheek, just below her eye. The wound was bleeding and the minnow, still on the hook, was struggling in the blood. An electric jolt of fear and guilt raced through me as I took in what I'd done to the person I cared about most. *How could I have been so careless*?! I released the drag on the reel and put the rod down and went to her. Stifling panic, as I'd seen her do in similar situations, I examined her cheek to see if the barb had buried. It hadn't, thank god! I lifted the hook out of the wound. With my folded T-shirt and pressure I stopped the bleeding.

My angry negligence invited punishment under the laws of karma and I've been punished all my life. That hook so close to my mother's eye is an image that hasn't softened or diminished with the years. Always the question is, what if I'd gone ahead and cast? When I'm really down, or upset, or feeling guilty, the whole scene can return in painful detail as I relive it, cringing.

THIRTY-SIX

ONE night when I was expecting to meet Katy at the rink she didn't show. Life in her family could be unpredictable so I understood, but I was disappointed. Public sessions without her were a yawn. Late in the evening Luke appeared and motioned me over to where he stood behind the rail. "Got a minute?" he asked. I followed him up into the bleachers on my toe stops to a spot he chose, high enough for a private conversation. Unflappable Luke seemed a little unsure of himself that night and more serious than I'd seen him before. I wondered if it was about Katy. He cleared his throat and began. "Gloria asked me to explain something we think you should know." His forehead bunched as he continued, "I'm probably not the right guy for this but I said I would."

For sure it was about Katy. With a sinking feeling, I waited.

He explained that girls grow up at different speeds mentally just as they do physically. "Some grow up fast because they want to be women, and others take longer because they're not quite ready to be women. Am I making sense?"

"Yes." He was making sense—and making me uncomfortable.

"Katy happens to be somebody that wants to go a little slower. But she *is* growing up. She loves you, Bill, and if you can wait a year or so she's going to be everything you want. She just needs a little more time to feel like a woman." After a pause and a quick glance at my face he said, "Anyway, maybe you'll think about it."

I said I would. How could I *not* think about it? I'd just learned my lovemaking put Katy off. It put her off so much she'd called in reinforcements.

"I know you love her," Luke said.

"Yes."

"That's why I'm not worried about you two. You'll figure it out. Anyway, thanks for listening."

We parted then, both embarrassed.

I wondered why Katy hadn't said anything to me. If she'd only spoken up I was sure I would have stopped pawing her. She'd chosen instead to expose her ten-fingered Romeo to others. I was embarrassed that Gloria and Luke knew our problems but I wasn't upset with them. They were only trying to help little sister. It was little sister who irked me.

I was irked with myself too. I should have noticed that my seductive techniques had become if not obnoxious to Katy, at least undesired. There were signs after all. Katy's need to "fall asleep" before being petted was a rather large sign. Unfortunately I hadn't bothered to read it. I was too intent on finding the techniques needed to draw out my girlfriend's amorous side.

In light of Luke's new information I decided my best course of action was inaction, a strict hands-off policy. If Katy wanted to be petted in the future she'd have to do it herself—or put in a request.

THIRTY-SEVEN

B Y the summer of 1961 Mother had survived a heart attack and breast cancer, and although Dad was healthy he was in his sixties. He worried that his sons might be left without parents before we were old enough to fend for ourselves. Always a planner, he asked one of his younger brothers and his wife to be our guardians in reserve. John and I had gotten to know and like Uncle Eliot, Aunt Cecelia, and their three boys during visits we'd made to our grandmother's farm in the Florida Panhandle while we were growing up. When I was sixteen and my brother thirteen, we were invited to Pensacola to stay with our possible future family for a week. Call it a test run.

We rode south on several Continental Trailways buses while I read *Gone with the Wind*, a book I'd often heard praised. I bought the thick paperback hoping for an entertaining story and also to learn more about the South and its people so I could fit in better down there. The social rules in Dixie seemed more complex and less rational than those I'd learned in Kansas, and during previous Florida visits I'd made some embarrassing blunders.

Margaret Mitchell's novel drew me in, giving me that good feeling you get when you begin a long book and realize it's going to hold your interest. I read while there was daylight, usually sitting next to my brother. As night filled the bus most of the passengers in the rear seats moved forward, perhaps responding to a primordial urge to be near the headlights. This left the darker half of the vehicle to John and me. We tried out all the empty seats just for the heck of it and when we felt sleepy we stretched out on the express's long rear cushion, comfortable accommodation for two adolescents laid end to end. The only drawback was the swaying and bouncing that happened behind the rear wheels. We handled that as most teens would, learning to snooze while being tossed around like two logs at the sawmill.

At our relatives' contemporary four-bedroom limestone my brother and I settled into our trial family. Every weekday morning Uncle Eliot, a good-humored newspaper publisher, shared breakfast with us then left for his press. Our oldest cousin, Ray Alan, home after his freshman year at the University of Florida, left next for his summer job at his dad's paper. Cousin Jerry, a year older than me, usually departed midmorning in his car to cruise the city and visit friends. And on most days my brother and I canoed with our youngest cousin Glen on the dark and deep Blackwater River, which flowed past the dock and boathouse at the bottom of their yard. Glen, ten or eleven at the time, was an unusually sweet-natured kid with a sandy crewcut combed up in front and a slow smile that rose from deep within. He had a lot of his mother in him and was widely loved in our extended family, as she was.

One morning Cousin Jerry invited me to go cruising with him. That surprised me. There had always been static of an undefined nature complicating our relationship, I think because we were close in age and both competitive. It didn't take me long to figure out that Jerry's parents had asked him to keep me entertained. I wasn't wild about that arrangement but told myself that if he and I spent time together we might learn to mesh better. That would be a plus if we later became brothers.

Jerry drove me over to his friend Beau's place, explaining on the way that he and Beau played football for Pensacola High. Jerry, a lineman, was proud of his team and expected them to win the conference championship and maybe go undefeated during the coming season. In an older subdivision he pulled into the driveway of a small tract home and honked. Beau emerged not from the house but from a weathered Airstream trailer parked at the end of his family's spottily grassed backyard. He walked with a fullback's swagger to the car and climbed in front next to me, depressing the seat springs. His big close-cropped head rested almost neckless on a muscular body in a shrunken T-shirt and faded blue jeans.

As we toured the streets of Pensacola my cousin and Beau talked across me, catching up on news. Beau confided he was recovering from the kegger he'd thrown in his trailer the night before. He'd gotten "righteously polluted" as had one of their high school classmates with an impressive bra size. Beau had talked her into spending the night. I learned that such parties were common in Beau's trailer and that Jerry often attended. Beau's parents, for purposes of domestic tranquility, had decided to ignore their seventeen-year-old son's amusements in his aluminum castle as long as he and his friends didn't bring down the fuzz.

Jerry razzed Beau for trying to nail all the "pushovers" at their high school. Beau razzed Jerry for getting busted. It came out that my cousin had been caught by a clerk in a sporting goods store while trying to pass one of the counterfeit twenties he'd printed on the linotype at his dad's paper. As the two bad boys recounted their wild lives, I realized they were trying to blow the mind of Billy Hayseed. And I guess they did. I couldn't help being impressed by how fast teens grew up on the Florida coast. Jerry and Beau were only a year older than me.

A day or two later Jerry invited me on a double date with his girlfriend and her younger sister. I accepted immediately. For two years I'd been so devoted to Katy I hadn't even thought about spending time with another girl, but recent events had weakened my fascination with my steady. An evening with a new girl appealed to me, if only to see what that was like. I figured she'd be about half as cute as Katy and not as interesting—and that would be that. After dinner the following evening I pulled on my newest jeans and my best shirt (a black and white polo) and slapped on an extra layer of cologne. Noticing Katy's name bracelet on my wrist, I thought it might be best to stow it in my suitcase for safe keeping. I felt a little guilty, but more than that I felt excited. I knew my date *might* be cute.

It was dusk and the streetlights were on as we drove to pick up the girls. Jerry mentioned casually that his girlfriend Miriam would be starting the University of Florida in the fall. I wondered how he'd gotten a girl a year ahead of him in school to take him seriously. Things like that didn't happen in my world. I was glad to hear that my date, Yasmin, was my age and like me would be a junior come fall.

On the outskirts of Pensacola we entered a far-flung subdivision so new its trees were skinny saplings. The neighborhood gave the feeling of wide open space under a big sky. Jerry parked in front of one of the small brick homes, virtually identical to those around it, and we got out and climbed the porch steps. He rang the doorbell. When our dates came out I could not believe my eyes. Standing in front of me were two utterly gorgeous women, both wearing white homecoming dresses that promoted well their superbly curvy figures. I was so blindsided by their glamour that when Jerry introduced me all I could manage was a breathless "Hi" for each sister.

Either of those girls, had they been old enough, could have filled a *Playboy* foldout to the satisfaction of the most discriminating connoisseur. They were blessed with different kinds of beauty, however. The long sable hair and soft almond eyes of Jerry's girlfriend Miriam conveyed sensuality and passivity. Her behavior was restrained, her movements languid. She seemed made to please. My date Yasmin had a sharper look, calling to mind the fictional heroine I'd developed a crush on as I rode south on the bus, the steel-willed mistress of Tara. Yasmin was a redhead with proud green eyes and a shapely, confident mouth that seemed aware some men would probably kill to kiss it. As I would learn, she was quick witted and verbally adroit and more to my taste than her less dynamic older sister.

Jerry took us to a miniature golf course and our game opened with him holding his girlfriend's wrists from behind and guiding her strokes like a horny golf pro. Meanwhile I was scrambling mentally to come up with the hilarious quip that would make my date howl while revealing my reserve of inner cool. I *desperately* wanted Yasmin to like me, just because she was such an absolute knockout.

As the four of us shifted positions over a hole, I saw Jerry and my date exchange a look of deep and amused complicity, one that suggested to me they knew each other a lot better than they should. I was shocked by the level of betrayal involved in that scenario, but had to wonder again how Jerry did it. If I was reading things right he was romancing two of the most desirable girls in his city, one behind the back of the other—and they were sisters! Jerry's looks, average at best, couldn't explain it. Was it his commitment to testing limits?

It was after ten when we left the miniature golf course. Jerry found a freeway and drove us out of town. Soon we were rolling on a long causeway with water not far below. The heavy smell of brine hung in the air. We traveled above the sea for many miles as traffic thinned to next to nothing—then it was nothing, just us flying on new concrete as the tires whined on rain grooves. Far from the city, with land under us again, Jerry exited the causeway and tooled down a short asphalt road to an empty parking lot.

As we walked through low dunes I began hearing the surf. Then I saw small breakers rolling in on what had to be the Gulf of Mexico. We were on the seaward side of Santa Rosa Island—next stop south the Yucatan.

Jerry told my date and me that he and Miriam were going for a walk. They strolled away on wet sand next to the breakers holding hands and carrying their shoes. On dry beach just above the slide of the waves Yasmin and I sat down. She pulled off her shoes and pushed her toes into the sand. I took off my shoes intending to do the same, then balked, leaving on my socks because I didn't want to get sand stuck between my toes, a rather silly worry it seems to me today. Naturally enough, Yasmin asked why I'd left my socks on. I didn't want to tell her the truth because it sounded ridiculous, so I told her I'd probably take them off later. That must have amused her but she was too kind to show it.

We talked about the things sixteen year olds usually talk about while getting acquainted, school and personal interests. My mind, and I think hers too, was really on something else. My date was sitting with her knees bent and in the dim light I could see the lean undersides of her thighs, those of a girl who probably played tennis. No way to miss the dramatic thrust of her chest. Or her breasts swelling against her scoop. Or her proud lips, waiting...

I thought she wanted me to kiss her but I wasn't sure. I found her a little intimidating. I'd never kissed a girl other than Katy, and Yasmin's advanced physical development made me feel like a kid eyeing a supercharged Bugatti he wasn't sure he knew how to start. I was inhibited as well by that private look I'd seen pass between my date and Jerry. It told me that in an important way Yasmin was my cousin's girl, one of his chicks. I expected her to tell him later about every stupid thing that I did. A lot stood in the way of our first kiss.

I remember our conversation being a little rocky at first, probably because I didn't really trust her. But it smoothed out as we talked. While we didn't always agree, we knew our own minds and were both articulate, so we began connecting. I learned she hoped to become a National Merit semifinalist during her junior year, as I did. That meant we were fellow nerds. She certainly didn't look like a nerd, but who other than our strange breed dreams of acing a standardized test? In time Jerry and Miriam reappeared walking slowly toward us. His arm was around her and she was leaning into him. Up close they looked rumpled and content. Jerry said it was time to start back.

On the drive to town I found out Yasmin was a reader. Books seemed a promising area for us to explore. I asked what kind she liked.

"Well, I liked *Hawaii*. Have you read it?

I'd tried to read James Michener's novel but soon found myself so bogged down in historical exposition I began skipping through its perhaps too numerous pages in search of the erotic scenes, some of which I'd sampled before purchase. The scenes were developed in enough titillating detail to be racy for the times, and this in my opinion was the book's main draw with readers, including me. My problem with the book, beyond its lengthy author talk, was that too often the characters and their dialogue rang false. However, I didn't want to alienate Yasmin by knocking something she admired, so I told her I'd liked the book. That was true in a way—I'd gotten a buzz from the cheesecake—but she must have noticed that my enthusiasm was lukewarm.

It was my turn to name a book I liked. I searched my mind for the perfect choice. Trying a little too hard, I guess, I came up with one I thought couldn't miss. It was a literary masterpiece, a work of genius deeply respected by everyone knowledgeable about great books. Those who'd read it, loved it—or at least said they did. With the most confidence I'd felt all evening I told her, "*David Copperfield.*"

I could see my date was not impressed. "What did you like about it?" she asked pointedly. The flinty look in her captivating green eyes told me she'd not only read the book but was prepared to debate. She had me cornered. What I liked about the novel was that everyone agreed it was wonderful, so I thought she would too. But she didn't, and she was being honest about it, unlike me. I remembered that in fact I'd found *David Copperfield* a long, hard, slog up a muddy hill. Doubtless it had promoted beneficial social causes in its day, but the writing is wordy and sentimental and reading it brought me not enjoyment but rather a small chip on my shoulder for having conquered a challenging literary peak. I was on shaky ground indeed when it came to explaining my admiration for my favorite book. Mercifully, I've forgotten my fraudulent arguments.

Back at the sisters' house, my cousin and Miriam stayed in the car to say goodnight while I walked Yasmin to her porch. There we stood, both uncomfortable. I knew it was my last chance to make up for not kissing her on the beach and I knew that the end of a date more or less required a kiss, but all the things that had inhibited me earlier inhibited me still, and now there were four curious eyes watching my every goofy move from the car. After considerable beating around the bush I thanked Yasmin for the date and held out my hand. Yes, dear reader, it's true. We shook hands and exchanged polite thank yous as chastely as Little Lord Fauntleroy and Miss Teenage America. Before I knew it the vision of loveliness I'd failed to engage was safe inside her house and her storm door was pulling itself closed. I descended the porch steps furious with myself yet trying to act nonchalant for Jerry and Miriam.

Long after Ray Alan fell asleep across the room from me, I lay awake raking through the ashes of my date and berating myself for letting Yasmin slip though my fingers totally untouched. If only I'd kissed her on the beach, I thought, she probably would have kissed me back and from there, who knew? I realized too late that her choice of Michener's book was not a literary judgment, but a hint she was interested in the same steamy scenes that interested me. As to Yasmin's probable involvement with Jerry, did that matter? I wasn't going to fall in love with her, was I? I wasn't planning to be her boyfriend. I just wanted to go with her where Katy wouldn't go with me. And for that, who better than Yasmin? Before I fell asleep I made up my mind to try again with her. I knew the mistakes I'd made. All I had to do was avoid those mistakes and our second date would unfold according to expectations—I hoped.

Since Jerry had set me up with Yasmin originally, I thought he might do it again. The next morning, less embarrassed than I should have been, I asked him if he would. He looked surprised but quickly covered it up. He wrote Yasmin's phone number on a piece of paper and told me my best chance of catching her was late in the afternoon. *Of course*, I thought, I'll call her up *myself*, the personal touch, what a dynamite idea! No wonder Jerry was so good with girls. I worked up my nerve all day and then while my aunt was starting dinner and no one was in the living room I made the call, armed with nothing more than trembling hands and a shaking voice. Yasmin sounded surprised to hear from me. I bumbled through my heavily rehearsed invitation to a movie I'd found in the paper, a movie I lacked a car to drive us to. I also lacked the driver's license required to operate the vehicle I didn't have. Yasmin must have pitied me as I displayed my catastrophic incompetence as a dater. She was really quite sweet about it though. She assured me she did very much want to see me, but when we tried to find a time it turned out she was booked air tight all the remaining days and nights of my Florida visit. She shut me down so gently it wasn't till long after I got off the phone that I understood what had happened.

I figured that was the end of my dating on the trip, revealing once again my abysmal ignorance of Southern society despite my continuing research in *Gone with the Wind*. The same evening Yasmin blew me off, my Aunt Cecelia made some phone calls that began buzzing switchboards all over the west Florida Panhandle where I couldn't throw a pinecone without hitting a relative on my father's side. The next morning an aunt of mine over in Pace reported in to headquarters. The daughter of a friend was staying with her, a girl who seemed to answer the needs admirably. Loralee, age fourteen and from Mobile, apparently wanted to meet me. We would be going swimming at a lake near Pace that afternoon.

Loralee was awfully cute with inquisitive brown eyes and thick mahogany hair that fell to her shoulder blades. Her erect, slim-hipped figure made me wonder about her breasts, too big one would think for a girl so young and lean. Her behavior, at first, seemed a little strange. I thought she was avoiding me, yet following me. When we got in my aunt's car to go to the lake, she climbed in next to me then looked out her window all the way, showing me the back of her head. And when we debarked at the lake in our swimsuits she walked off and I lost sight of her. Are we with each other, I wondered, or not.

I was sitting on the dock after my first dive, dripping and feeling lonely, when I looked down and there she was below my feet, standing chest deep in the lake and staring out over the water at nothing in particular. It occurred to me this might be her way of getting to know a guy, making herself available while acting noncommittal. I asked the top of her head "How is it down there?" And she looked up and answered. Soon she was sitting beside me on the dock and we were deep in conversation. After that we were inseparable.

Loralee liked to talk, which took the pressure off me. I listened as she described her eventful life in Mobile, her very cool girl-friends, her nineteen-year-old steady, her steady's fast car, and the blast that awaited her in ninth grade. Her unselfconscious bragging was seasoned with an endearing dash of bravado, cal-culated to impress, I could tell. I didn't believe everything she said but was quite pleased she thought me worth impressing.

This girl was just the confidence booster I needed in the after-math of Yasmin. Loralee was even less assured than me, making me feel more mature. She was a cheerful, slightly kooky girl with a winning personality and as we talked I found myself liking her a lot. I guess she felt the same way because after dinner she led me onto the front porch and beneath a 60-watt bulb bumped by mesmerized flying critters we made out in a porch swing. Between kisses Loralee kept looking over her shoulder through the front window, obviously worried about someone watching. I suggested we move to my aunt's car parked away from the house under a magnolia.

We got in the front seat and ran down the windows, letting in a faint breeze and scores of mosquitos. The mosquitos were chew-ing us up pretty good but we ignored them and entered lip-lock mode. Loralee was a good kisser, more down to earth than Katy yet still quite sweet, and I thought I was really getting somewhere with her—exploring new territory. But she was remarkably adept at redirecting a roving hand on the verge of discovery and when my aunt called from the porch to tell me my ride was on the way, I realized I hadn't gone anywhere with her I hadn't already been. I hadn't even found out whether her amazing breasts were real. Given the sophistication of her evasive maneuvers and the quality of her kisses, I decided she might indeed have a nine-teen-year-old boyfriend. While Katy was a little slow for me and Yasmin too fast, Loralee was just my speed.

Riding back to Wichita on the bus I finished *Gone with the*

Wind and did a lot of thinking. The two somewhat boy-crazy "Southern belles" I'd met in Florida had without a doubt turned my head. In the words of that song from the First World War, "How ya gonna keep 'em down on the farm after they've seen Paree?" My time with Yasmin and Loralee had convinced me my relationship with Katy was basically juvenile. Naturally, my girlfriend lost glamour in my eyes.

It was the most amazing transformation. For two years I'd been obsessed with Katy. My feelings for her had been as strong as ever right up until I visited Florida, and now those feelings were numb. Such a swift and radical change of heart bothered me because it suggested I was fickle, not the way I wanted to view myself. Yet, at the same time, my disenchantment with my steady allowed me to imagine life with a girlfriend more my own speed, an elating prospect. I began to think there must be girls like Yasmin and Loralee back home—really cute girls eager to become women. Once that bee was in my bonnet I couldn't get it out.

THIRTY-EIGHT

O N my first visit to the Alaskan after my Florida trip I felt I was returning to a place I'd known years earlier. The rink was scruffier than I remembered and seemed quaint, a world that hadn't moved on. Katy, sporting the same old ponytail, bangs and plaid bermudas hadn't moved on either. She was exactly the way I'd left her except that she seemed paler—paler certainly than the Southern girls I'd been hobnobbing with. My steady looked me over with concerned eyes, taking in my world-class tan, a composite of five or six deep sunburns laid down one on top of the other. I was brown as a medium-roast coffee bean. When I told her about my trip south I mentioned the long bus ride, canoeing the Blackwater with little Glen, and Cousin Jerry's counterfeit twenties—but I didn't mention Yasmin or Loralee or that I'd stowed a certain symbolic name bracelet in my suitcase. Katy listened in silence, looking like she didn't quite know what to make of the new browner and more self-assured me.

When we joined a couples skate, I found the ritual in place but stripped of its magic. Skating hand in hand to the familiar music struck me as tame and repetitive, forever leading back to where we'd been. In my mind's eye I could see Jerry and Miriam and Yasmin watching my fifteen-year-old steady and me as we pursued our roller thrills in the company of actual *children*. How hilarious we must look, and how pathetic! My social life in Kansas, centered at the rink, had become an embarrassment.

Later, I was skating by myself in the revolving crowd during a free skate when someone called my name. Lauren McCabe was waving me over. She sat in a folding chair in the mouth of the exit tunnel, putting on her skates. The rear door guard had a crush on Lauren so she was welcome in his domain any time and often hung out there. I rolled off the floor and stopped in front of her and said hi.

"How'd you get so tan?" she asked. I told her pretty much what I'd told Katy, again neglecting to mention the girls I'd met in Florida. As we talked, Lauren leaned forward over her skates and resumed lacing, providing me a stimulating view down her blouse where two shapely breasts hung half unholstered from their white cotton C cups. I was taking mental snapshots when she looked up and caught my eyes. Lauren's eyes were her best feature—wideset, strikingly blue, and full of fun. She gave me a big smile, and when I smiled back, I felt a hard tap on my shoulder. I turned to find Katy dangling my name bracelet, which she promptly dropped. I caught it on the way down as she skated away.

I took my sweet time finishing my conversation with Lauren. If Katy didn't like it—too bad. Only when Lauren and I ran out of things to talk about did I skate back to my girlfriend at the other end of the floor. I felt like I'd had it with her. Our long-running breakup drama was now tiresome to me and I couldn't find much reason for us to be together. She was sitting on the bench where she and I put on and took off our skates and where we usually spent time together. It was the bench my brother and I had claimed during our first days at the rink. Katy had joined us there after she became my girlfriend. Now she sat in the middle of "our bench" alone, looking defeated. She may have guessed what was coming. I rolled up to the rail in front of her and stepped over. Standing beside her I returned her bracelet and said in a calm voice, "Katy, all we do is fight. Let's break up for good this time."

I thought she'd assume I was playing our old game and get mad, as usual. However, I saw no anger in her face. Stoicism had set in like a winter freeze. Only her eyes revealed what was going on inside her—and they said she was hurt, almost defenseless. Although I'd become bored with her, apparently she wasn't yet bored with me.

She stood up on her skates, turned her back to me and rolled to the end of the bench. There she stopped. She was facing away, not moving, and I wondered what she was up to when in a couple of quick heaves she threw up her dinner on the floor at her feet. She stepped around it on her toe stops and skated off in the direction of the restrooms.

I wanted to clean it up. I'd caused it and the sight of it made me feel guilty. Cleaning up though meant going to the men's room for paper towels and possibly bumping into Katy, so I left the problem behind by skating to another bench where I changed into my shoes. I walked home under gently stirring summer leaves filtering the glow of streetlights as I thought over what had happened. I recalled that during my walk to the rink earlier I hadn't planned to break up with Katy. I'd been looking forward to seeing her after our longest separation. Yet when the opportunity arose to end our relationship, I'd grabbed it.

At first I didn't understand why Katy took the breakup so hard. Then I realized that if she'd dropped me a month earlier, when she was still at the center of my world, I'd have been destroyed. She had no idea what had happened to me in Florida to change my feelings and must have been caught flatfooted by my decision. My explanation, "All we do is fight," wasn't much of one.

I did believe I'd done the right thing. The part of me Katy

didn't want to deal with was a part I wanted to explore, and I thought if we tried to keep something going when its time had passed she'd keep getting hurt. Also, I'd become skeptical of the turbulent passion we'd shared for two unforgettable years. What we thought was love looked to me now more like puppy love. We believed it was something greater because it was so powerful. But it must have been infatuation. Otherwise, how could I have fallen out of it so fast? Confident in my decision, I tried to push Katy from my mind. Thinking about her just made me feel bad.

THIRTY-NINE

'D given up speed skating, and Katy too, but I still had a reason to visit the Alaskan. I wanted to get to know Lauren better. She'd always been friendly to me and I thought she might be interested in me. Certainly I'd become interested in her. She was pretty, with a spherical auburn bouffant, those arresting blue eyes, and a smile that was bright and winning even though one of her incisors was out of alignment. She was almost seventeen then and knew how to dress to promote her trim, well-appointed figure and how to tastefully underline her natural good looks with makeup. Among girls at the rink near my age only Katy was more attractive—and that judgment depended on one's taste in beauty. If you went for the angelic look, you'd definitely choose Katy. But if you preferred a more earthy presentation you might pick Lauren. Lauren's sultry charms made me think she might be the right speed for the guy I wanted to become.

There were promising things I knew about Lauren. Rick Shafer had dated her for several months and he only dated girls he thought he could get into bed. He admitted he hadn't quite succeeded with Lauren but was convinced she'd slept with the guy she went with after him—somebody a year or two older than us. Lauren had dumped Rick to date that guy, then later she got dumped. As far as Rick knew, she was still unattached.

I returned to the Alaskan on an evening when I guessed Lauren might be there and Katy probably wouldn't. I guessed right, and after some hesitation I asked Lauren to join me for a couples skate. She was surprised but accepted. I couldn't tell whether she was pleased or not. It was strange skating with someone new. Lauren and I were a little out of sync and her weight on my arm felt sluggish compared to Katy's. Both Lauren and I were tense.

When the house lights came up, we stayed on the floor together cruising with the crowd and talking as we tried to relax. I learned she was in the Pep Club at West High and was majoring in biology/physiology and that she had a part-time job with a furrier, which paid for her clothes. She was big on clothes and gave a lot of thought to what she wore. I was disappointed to learn she was almost two months older than me and would have been a year ahead in school if she hadn't missed so many days with polio in the third grade that she'd had to repeat. But I knew such a small age difference wasn't a good reason not to date her. When we ran out of things to talk about she kept the conversation going with a monologue as she narrated, almost frame by frame, the plot of a movie she'd seen.

While Lauren droned on I suffered such monumental boredom that just remembering it makes me sleepy. Couldn't she hear herself? And why was she so nervous? Then I noticed members of the speed club watching us. Some were in the bleachers taking us in as we rolled by and others were circling the floor with us, sneaking looks through the crowd. In different faces I saw several different reactions—surprise, disapproval, amusement, disgust. It wasn't their business who I skated with, so I tried to ignore them, but Lauren was buckling under the social pressure. She and Katy had never liked each other and Katy had far more clout at the rink.

Eventually the plot of Lauren's movie came to an end and film flapped in the projector as we searched for something else to talk about. When we couldn't come up with anything, she begged off to visit the ladies. I didn't bother her again until the end of the session when I asked her to join me for the last skate. Maybe because the rink was dark then, she accepted. This time we were a little less tense. After the skate ended I asked her if she wanted to meet me at a session later in the week and we decided on a night.

When Lauren didn't show that night, I was very let down. I visited the Alaskan a couple more times hoping to run into her but didn't. I concluded she wasn't really interested in me and gave up chasing her. In fact, I gave up on girls. I returned to my earlier life, the one I'd lived until Katy came along late in the summer after eighth grade and transformed me from a bumpkin to a boyfriend. Without great regret I confined myself to the safe and comfortable world of my school buddies and my family and became a nerd in the slow lane again.

FORTY

NLIKE the adolescent male of American myth I was in no hurry to drive a car. I think I was reluctant to take on so much responsibility. I had a sense I might not be good at driving and was afraid of accidents. In school assemblies I'd seen films showing the aftermath of horrific car wrecks with blood and bodies everywhere, so I knew what could happen almost too well. Getting hurt myself was one thing, but what really worried me was hurting other people and their expensive vehicles, not to mention knocking our family ride out of service and jacking our insurance premium. For months after I turned sixteen I put off getting a driver's license.

As time went by though it became more embarrassing to ask my parents for rides. And since I planned to find a new girl-friend someday, I needed to be ready for dates beyond the rink. Fresh in my mind was my bungle in the jungle of Florida's dating scene, when I'd invited a girl to a movie without being able to get us there. Most of my buddies were driving happily and I was nearly the last man out when I finally capitulated, joining the vast majority of my fellow Americans in their commitment to vehicle mastery. I asked my mother to teach me how to drive.

One Sunday afternoon, on the wide expanse of an empty

Sears & Roebuck parking lot, in our family's column-shift 1958 Ford Fairlane, Mom guided me through releasing the emergency brake, depressing the clutch and dropping the transmission into first. I was hopping with the heebie-jeebies as I eased up on the clutch and the engine jerked us forward twice, coughed hard, and died. After several tries, with Mom explaining how to do it and me screwing up, I got so frustrated and overwrought that she bailed on the project and drove me home. Next Dad gave it a shot. His first lesson kicked off with us circling the block in first gear as we debated how to shift into second, then he bailed—putting me back on square one.

My parents learned from friends that their son had been taught to drive by a sergeant with the Wichita Police Department. This veteran instructor came highly recommended and we decided to give him a try. I think my folks assumed I wouldn't have the brass to fly in the face of a police sergeant.

Sergeant Rossler turned out to be a well upholstered middle-aged lawman with an inventor's soul—and his soul was on fire. His brain child was a consolidated accelerator/brake pedal that shortened the time it takes a driver to brake. It functioned as an accelerator when depressed and as a brake when released. The sergeant was convinced it would someday be adopted worldwide, saving thousands if not millions of lives each year. He believed in it so fervently he'd had one installed on his squad car. If I understood him correctly (I couldn't believe I did) I was going to learn to drive using his questionable contraption. The sergeant and I were sitting together in his cruiser in front of our house when he pressed the footfeed and we departed the curb just as in any car with an automatic transmission. Halfway down the block he eased up on his miracle pedal and the brakes engaged, slowing us smoothly to a stop. "See," he said. "Simple."

Indeed I saw. I saw the sergeant was a little balmy. He was proposing to teach me to drive on equipment I doubted I'd ever use again. Worse, his invention seemed dangerous for the very reason he loved it—it combined contrary functions. There is a point in having two pedals, one to go forward and one to stop. It separates two very different mechanical outcomes in a driver's mind. I didn't share these doubts with my instructor, but I did warn myself to keep an eye on him. A guy like that can be full of surprises.

We stopped and traded places so I could drive. Despite my lack of faith in the sergeant's invention I found it easy to use. Pressing down to go forward and easing up to brake, I followed his directions as he took us up Hillside to Douglas, then west on Douglas past businesses and the East High campus into downtown, where late evening traffic flowed under streetlights. Retail stores glowed brightly, open for late shoppers among darkened office buildings. Piloting the sergeant's deep-throated and responsive cruiser so empowered me that my main challenge became holding the speed limit.

At times I was distracted by Sergeant Rossler's pronouncements on various topics unrelated to our mission. He had many opinions, all of them definite, and I had to listen to them carefully because his driving instructions were woven seamlessly into his editorials on human folly. In the middle of downtown, as he tediously unpacked some kernel of wisdom, his order to turn left came a bit late. This meant I entered the left turn lane late and had to hit the brakes. Instinctively I pressed *down* on the accelerator instead of easing up. The vehicle surged forward as we bore down on an immense concrete traffic island that ended the turn lane decisively with an immovable object. "Stop! Stop! Stop!" screamed the sergeant. His extreme urgency and the high pitch of his alarm spooked me and I mashed the pedal harder and the car leapt again. With a quickness I wouldn't have thought he possessed, the sergeant grabbed my leg with both hands and yanked it off the accelerator. His patrol car squalled to a halt, throwing us forward into our seatbelts. Accident averted. His amazing pedal had just saved two lives.

"*Didn't you hear me say STOP?!*" the sergeant demanded, incensed.

"I was trying to stop."

"You know what? I'm gonna get a pin for you so I can stick you to wake you up. Yeah, that's *exactly* what I'm gonna do." He had a point. My mind did tend to wander, especially when encouraged to.

The sergeant kept threatening me with that pin during our remaining lessons, all conducted in our family Ford rather than his official vehicle, maybe because he didn't want to put city property at risk again. The lessons went smoothly. The last one ended with an emergency braking test on the open highway. I was told to drive out of town past Beech Aircraft's production facilities humming brightly on second shift. Some miles beyond, in the pitch dark countryside, my teacher told me to take it up to seventy. With asphalt racing at us under the headlights, he said to hit the brakes.

He'd prepared me well for this crucial moment. I knew to *not* slam the brake pedal, but rather to apply firm consistent pressure. Looming in my mind was the sergeant's grisly anecdote about a former female student. In a car without seatbelts (like the one we were riding in) she'd hit the brakes so hard she was thrown into the roof, crushing her skull "like an eggshell" and "dying instantly." On that occasion the sergeant presumably was spared a similar fate by the greater gravitational force holding him down to the seat. I followed his advice carefully, passed my last test with flying colors, and for once my teacher was satisfied with my alertness.

After Sergeant Rossler signed off on me, he presented me with the imaginary pin, saying, "Hang onto this because you're going to need it." Since he'd just certified me as a qualified Kansas driver

I didn't take him too seriously. But in the years that followed I was involved in a worrying series of fender benders. Although only vehicles got hurt, my wandering mind set me up for all of them. At age twenty-two, after my seventh minor crash, a scary one on the highway, I learned to use my pin whenever I drove.

FORTY-ONE

I N early autumn of 1961 a friend of my mother's gave me a life-changing gift. Yvonne was what we'd call a trophy wife today. She'd been a counter clerk in a downtown department store when she met the man she would marry, fifteen years her senior and well on his way to becoming one of our city's most powerful businessmen. At the time I write of, Yvonne was in her forties and still very attractive, with sympathetic, vulnerable, deep eyes. Unfortunately, her marriage wasn't happy. She told her troubles to my mother and sometimes Mom would pass along heavily abridged versions to me. I knew Yvonne's husband from holiday dinners our families shared and he'd always seemed a gentleman, cordial and mild in tone. But he was an extremely confident man of high intelligence who chose his words carefully and I didn't doubt he could punch hard with his mouth. Mom wasn't one to air anyone's dirty laundry, but in this case her purpose seems clear. She wanted me to learn how *not* to treat a woman.

I'm pretty sure Mother unburdened herself to Yvonne in return, not about her marriage but about me—her moody, impulsive, agnostic, vandalizing son who was himself capable of throwing a damaging verbal punch. In some ways Yvonne had come to

WILLIAM HART

understand me better than my mother and her gift proved it. At the end of a visit to her house, as the three of us were moving toward the front door, she asked us to wait. She stepped into their den and pulled a hardback from a bookshelf, then brought it out and started to hand it to me. But after a glance at Mom's face she pulled the book to her chest and held it so I could see the title—a title as strange and mysterious as they come. "I'm not sure you're ready for this," she said, "so maybe I shouldn't give it to you. But I wanted you to know about it."

That same day I drove downtown to Rector's and bought a copy of the book, a new Signet paperback costing fifty cents. The years have reduced that book to a sheaf of loose pages cradled between two tattered covers but I've kept it because I love it and because it marks the beginning of my permanent devotion to literature.

When the copy was new I opened it in the privacy of my bedroom while sitting up in bed with a pillow behind me. A small tube light clamped to the top of my headboard lit my way. At first I wasn't sure I liked the book. It was so different from anything I'd read before that I didn't know quite what to make of it. A guy exactly my age was talking—talking and cussing. His voice was so real I felt I was hearing him speak. He seemed a little weird but he was unusually truthful and that made me begin to trust him. His skill in reading people was fascinating. Like me he evaluated others based on their behavior but his judgments were more insightful than mine.

I fell so completely under the sway of that messianic work of fiction that for a day and a half I forgot my world and lived in the narrator's. The experience was deeply emotional. I sweated and shivered and all but incandesced with nervous energy as I savored every page. The morning I finished I came down with a bad cold. As I reentered the nonfictional world I lived in, I noticed my outlook had changed. I was now alert for the phonies

202

in my daily life as I tried to avoid becoming one myself. Striving for complete transparency I turned simple questions needing simple answers into minor works of philosophical reflection. When I was around, questions like "Is my B.O. bad?" became dangerous to ask. Reading that novel was for me a spiritual experience. Its powerful argument for authenticity helped me refine my developing moral code.

The author also showed me the power of a profound story executed by a master. I began to dream of someday writing a book as real, one that affected readers as fundamentally as I'd been affected. That ambition, still with me, has probably always been beyond my gifts, but given my overbaked personality, I probably need a worthy but unattainable goal to orient my life.

I think Yvonne's reason for introducing me to the book was to convince me I wasn't alone in the world. The protagonist is fictional of course, but the mind that created him was both real and, at that time, alive somewhere in New England. The author's existence, along with my own, suggested a scattered tribe of malcontents like us out there, roaming the woods and coming through the rye. The book's popularity meant our tribe was larger than one might think. I did feel less alone.

Yvonne was a generation younger than my parents and that's likely why she intuited the book's rightness for me when my own mother couldn't. I learned later that Mom had read the novel but hadn't liked it. She thought its narrator was sadly disturbed. Not surprising really. Between her teen years and mine two generations of social change had happened. The youth-centric culture I grew up in was alien to both my parents, who were teens during the repressive, adult-dominated society of the First World War years. By 1960 a huge shift in social mores had snuck up on my folks from out of the future.

This generational disconnect might have been a problem for us if my parents hadn't had a safety valve. They'd made many friends in the generation between theirs and mine as they raised children with these younger couples—and sometimes these friends bridged the age gap in our family. During my early life a number of Yvonnes stepped in to help us. At least once though no one stepped in. That was when it came time for my parents to have "the talk" with me. There was no talk. Instead they presented me with a hardbound copy of 'Twixt Twelve and Twenty, Pat Boone's advice to teenagers on sex, a book that in its racier passages instructs how to control deep kisses and petting with tactical suppression. My folks wanted me to read the book then ask them about anything I didn't understand. I knew then that my sex education would happen with little input from them. To me that seemed a good thing. I felt fully capable of self-educating on this intriguing subject, having on my own dime gotten ahead of all my friends thanks to Katy. To me Pat Boone's prissy advice was a joke. Elvis's views on the same subject I might have taken more seriously.

FORTY-TWO

I N November Lauren phoned to say hi and to catch up. As we talked, she mentioned she was having trouble in American history, a required course for Kansas high school juniors. "How is your class going?" she asked. Since I'd helped her with math problems at the rink, I thought I saw where she was headed. I was a little disappointed that she was calling on the nerd in me rather than the part that liked girls, but I thought I might be able to help her. The textbook we were using in my honors class was several cuts above any history book I'd studied before. Its greater factual detail and more complex explanations of events made the story of my country interesting to me for the first time. Since I wanted to see Lauren anyway, I offered to let her take a look at my college-level text and keep it for a while if she chose. She invited me over to her house and gave me directions.

On the evening we picked, I drove from my eastside neighborhood west on Kellogg past the playing fields behind my high school then over the Wichita railyards and across the river to Lauren's inner city neighborhood a stone's throw from downtown. Among the small, well maintained one-story frame houses on her street I found the address. Her family's two bedroom shotgun with a finished attic and new roof was in excellent repair and had a nicely grassed front yard.

In a tidy living room that smelled of supper Lauren and I sat together on an overstuffed couch reading around in each other's history books. I remember being puzzled by the lack of content in Lauren's text. It was written at what seemed a seventh grade level and was so basic in information as to be almost meaningless. I wondered how two students in the same school system could be educated so differently. Was East High that much better than West, or was the difference explained by the higher expectations of my honors class?

Lauren wasn't as interested in my history book as I'd expected her to be. In fact, she seemed only moderately interested in school—and I realized I'd been conned. Her intelligence was more practical than academic, explaining why I was sitting next to her on her family's couch, lured across town under false pretenses. I didn't mind the subterfuge because it got us together, something both of us wanted, and I accepted Lauren's low-key attitude toward school just as I'd accepted Katy's. But with this new girl I was already missing the honesty I'd taken for granted in my first girlfriend. From day one I felt Lauren and I weren't always on the same wavelength.

I did like her positive disposition. She was happy and outgoing and easy to get along with. It was autumn so she was in her element, being built for sweaters. Her breasts were larger than average and very appealingly suspended, thanks to a high quality bra and a physical grace note courtesy of our creator. Without self-consciousness she sat so close to me on the couch that our knees touched and I was pleased to find her laughing at my witticisms. At the end of my visit I let her keep my history book not because I expected her to study it but so we would see each other again.

More than a week passed without me hearing from her. I was

falling behind in history when I came up with a plan to get my textbook back. I phoned Lauren and invited her to a movie, mentioning I could also pick up my book. She was with me all the way and so the following Friday or Saturday evening we found ourselves downtown at the Orpheum Theater. It was a cold, blustery night and the lobby was packed with young people in coats standing in a long line that snaked back and forth between red velvet ropes. As Lauren and I inched toward our tickets we drew even with a guy ahead of us whom Lauren knew. The two of them were very glad to see each other and dropped out of line for several minutes to talk while his date and I held their places. He turned out to be a friend of Lauren's from West, though she didn't say what kind of friend.

The film was "Town without Pity," a depressing story featuring gang rape and suicide. It left me sad and nauseated, not the ideal mood for a date. I thought food might settle my stomach so I drove to the Griff's on my side of town for hamburgers. We ate in the parking lot while seated in the car with the heater running. I think because she was nervous, Lauren began talking nonstop the way she had the first time we skated together. Her new subject was what she'd been up to with her girlfriends, who I didn't know and who didn't sound particularly fascinating. All I remember is that one of the girls had borrowed some of Lauren's LP records and got peanut butter on them and Lauren was pissed about it. As I pretended to listen, my neck stiffened and I began to wonder whether I wanted to date somebody who periodically bored me silly. I couldn't think of anything else to do on our date, so I drove Lauren back to the west side and parked in front of her house and *she was still talking*. It was time for me to kiss her but how was I supposed to do that with her mouth motoring on down the pike?

I thought maybe she needed a hint so I leaned her way and turned my face toward her. She stopped talking and swung her head to meet me. Clearly she'd been waiting. As we came together my tender kiss was engulfed by her wide open mouth. I opened my mouth to match hers and wrestled her tongue with mine, following her lead. To me it seemed too much too soon but I didn't want her to think I was a prude. During that kiss and those that followed my forehead pressed into her bouffant, stiff with hairspray and smelling of chemicals. Four kisses were enough for me. We said our good-byes and I drove home certain I wouldn't ask her out again. She wasn't my type. Not only was she not my type, but being with her made me miss Katy.

In the days that followed Lauren's kisses stayed with me as their meaning sank in. Weren't they an invitation to get to know her physically much better than I'd gotten to know my previous girlfriend? And wasn't that what I wanted? I decided it was foolish to let a little hairspray deflect me from my goal, so I phoned Lauren and asked her out again. That date went better, ending with more than four kisses, many more, and soon we were seeing each other regularly. As we put in time making out we adjusted our kisses to please both of us and I learned to ignore the hairspray. We went to movies, played pool, ate fast food, and watched TV, usually at my house where we had more privacy. Once we ice skated on an informal outdoor rink near where she lived, a bumpy patch of ice laid down on a baseball diamond with a garden hose.

The main purpose of our dates, for both of us I think, were the long good-byes. As the weeks passed and then the months she lowered her barriers one by one, allowing me to advance my petting around the bases. In November I divined the secrets of her enchanting chest. By Christmas my hands had mapped the rest of her. At some point during late winter we began having full sex. Usually I'd sit in the middle of the front seat and one of us would pull off her panties while her skirt stayed on to provide cover. She'd swing a leg over me, facing me as she sat on my lap.

I used a condom and because the latex reduced my sensitivity I sometimes had to plug away for ages to get off. My partner didn't seem to mind.

Not long after Lauren and I began making love she told me about an unusual injury she'd suffered in grade school. She'd fallen off a swing and ruptured her hymen. At first I couldn't understand why she was telling me this—and totally out of the blue—then realized it was her attempt to explain why I hadn't encountered a hymen the first time we'd had sex. Bless her heart, she wanted me to believe I'd taken her virginity. It was a thoughtful gesture, but Rick's story about an older boyfriend doing the deed seemed more plausible than the medically perplexing accident she reported. I didn't like being lied to about *that* particular matter and wondered how many other lies she'd told. Untruthfulness was definitely not something I wanted in a girlfriend. However, when I factored in the benefit of having a permissive partner—a highly permissive partner—I decided that if I could live with her hairspray, I could live with a smattering of her lies. Lying was perhaps something to be expected in a girl who was more compliant, a part of the bargain I'd made.

As Lauren and I continued to date we took our lovemaking to new locations. We did it on my family's rec room couch under Grandma's quilt with the TV going to cover our sounds. We did it standing up in the rec room bathroom. We did it on Lauren's backyard lawn with the family dog sniffing around us. And we almost did it underneath my trench coat in the rear seat of a Volvo while speeding down the Kansas Turnpike with another couple.

Our very physical romance was conducted with no great skill I think, certainly very little on my part, but with the energy and enthusiasm of the young. Lauren and I founded our relationship there—though not there entirely. As she relaxed around me her monologues dwindled and we enjoyed more two-way conversations. I came to see she lied only occasionally, when she thought it necessary, and as my trust in her grew we became friends. I kept a large and flattering framed photo of her on my dresser and began telling people she was my girl. I all but forgot about Katy, which wasn't hard because I didn't go to the Alaskan and never ran into her at East. Thinking about her just made me feel guilty.

During our speed club days Lauren had been a cautious racer and not very fast. Her reluctance to engage may have been why Katy and Gloria nicknamed her "Chicken." I'd assumed Lauren was mediocre in all sports until we began dating and I found contrary evidence staring me in the face. In tennis, although she couldn't handle my best serves, once we got into a game she held her own with good court coverage and well-placed returns. She used my quick feet against me, running me ragged. She won about one game in three and sometimes took a set, challenging me enough that our competitions were fun for both of us. In eight ball too she beat me about a third of the time. She had good pool vision and a straight, firm stroke. Sighting in she got her cheek right down on the stick, one big blue eye locked and loaded, her bridge a wadded fist with curlicue.

She played ping pong with her game face on and usually whipped me. Her hands were really quick, the kind of hands a professional pickpocket would die for. Many times I smashed a return I thought she couldn't possibly deal with only to see the ball come squarely off her paddle and drop on my side of the table. She gave me a better game than most guys.

Lauren was a highly agreeable date, pleased to do anything I suggested, happy just to be with me. As we spent time together I got better at making her laugh until I could really crack her up. It's nice being with a girl who appreciates your humor and shows it. Getting a laugh out of Katy had sometimes been like sparking flint. Not to say Katy was ever dull. Whenever I was in the same room with her I felt her presence like a form of gravity. Lauren didn't affect me that way, but she was more fun.

One of my new girlfriend's behaviors I found flattering, yet disconcerting. She tended to adopt my enthusiasms and make them her own. Reading books for example. Before meeting me she hadn't been much of a reader, but as we dated she became one. The first book I remember her getting interested in was Leon Uris's *Exodus*. When she found out I was reading it and liked it, she wanted to read it. Once I was done I loaned her my copy. After she read it, we went to see the movie. Other books followed, and over time more of my commitments became her commitments—like my agnosticism and my leftist politics. These commonalities brought us closer, but they spooked me too. It was like she was trying to live her life while looking over my shoulder and sometimes I wished she had more faith in her own identity. It wasn't that she was ashamed of her working-class background. Actually, she was proud of that. What she wanted, I think, was the ability to confidently navigate middle-class culture where she saw more opportunity to live life on her own terms and be freer than her mother had been.

Lauren's parents had grown up in a small Nebraska town where they became a couple and married. He was the best mechanic in the county, she one of the prettiest girls. Looking for a better life they moved to Wichita and Mr. McCabe got a good-paying job as a tool and die maker at one of the top machine shops in the city. When his company folded many years later, he started a lucrative business of his own—buying, repairing and reselling all manner of electronic equipment from stereos to color TVs. His edge was his ability to diagnose cheap fixes during the time before an auction, when bidders were allowed to inspect the sale items.

Mrs. McCabe had from her teen years been under the spell of Hollywood, immersed in movies, movie magazines, and an involving fantasy life. She named her baby daughter after her favorite actress, Lauren Bacall. According to baby daughter, the realities of marriage to a plain spoken and controlling working stiff clashed with her mother's beautiful dreams, pushing her into a major emotional collapse. Mrs. McCabe was hospitalized and given electroshock "therapy" until it broke her, turning her into a saccharine sweet Pollyanna with a penetrating voice. When I visited her home she loved me half to death, seeing to my every need real or imagined with about twice the overkill of my own too solicitous mom. Mrs. M. was a loving and well-meaning emotional bear hug.

FORTY-THREE

OUR parents began giving my brother and me small allowances around the time John started school. When Mom returned to teaching a few years later our allowances were increased to pay us for taking on the household chores. My allowance had usually been enough to cover my personal expenses, but dating Lauren soon had me running in the red. Once I'd drained my savings I started dipping into the solid silver half dollars my father was pulling out of circulation as an investment. Theft from a parent is bad news, and I did feel guilty, but I'd become so dependent on "dating" that, like most addicts, I let my morals slide to feed the addiction.

Condom procurement alone blew a hole in my budget. I was too young to buy them in stores, too shy as well, and the only rubber vending machine I knew about was bolted to the wall of a gas station men's room in Augusta, Kansas twenty miles away. That dispenser, decorated with garish and improbable guarantees of satisfaction and smudged by grubby hands, gouged mercilessly on price. Like most vending machines at that time, it took half dollars as well as quarters.

During my financial crisis one of my mother's many younger friends phoned to ask if I'd be interested in a job as stock boy at a pharmacy she managed. I'd be working a few hours after school several evenings a week at minimum wage. Just when I really needed it, here was the answer to my funding deficit. I grabbed the job and on a dismal winter evening a few days later I drove to the drugstore crunching frozen slush all the way. I'd learned to like Lenora during dinners our families had shared and was glad to see her warm smile as she welcomed me to the store and asked after my parents. My duties, she explained, would be to keep the shelves stocked and the products dusted. She introduced me to the pharmacist, Samuel, a tall, stooped man in his late thirties. Samuel's grizzled brown flat top dipped just perceptibly in my direction as he appraised me with deep-set critical eyes. His mouth seemed permanently turned down on one side, as though he expected to be irritated by whatever came next. Well, I told myself, let Samuel be Samuel. He's the store pharmacist and of minor concern. I'll be working for Lenora.

I didn't see Lenora again for months. Although she was credited with managing three stores, all owned by a certain Mr. Callaghan whom I never met, I wasn't really sure what her job was because she was never around. From my second day on I took orders from Samuel, who communicated with me exclusively in clipped phrases, all job related. While I restocked the shelves from a plastic basket he watched me closely and with apparent suspicion through the cross-hatched wire of his pharmaceutical enclosure. Was he afraid I was going to lift an enema kit or dip into the cold cream? The only items in that store of interest to me were the condoms, and those were locked up safely in Samuel's cage along with him and the narcotics. Aside from Samuel, my job was great. It required so little of my attention I could daydream endlessly.

One warm April evening Lenora reappeared at the store and approached me. She told me to put down my dust rag and come with her. Samuel scowled at us as I followed her out the back door and into the alley where we climbed into a late model Chrysler Imperial. Before she started the engine she commended me for doing my job so splendidly, just as she'd known I would, then added, "You'll be getting a small raise." Affecting a breezy manner she said she wanted to show me the other stores she managed—and off we went.

I couldn't help noticing that Lenora was all dolled up. Her hair was clipped behind her head in an attractive manner, exposing two very cute ears, and she wore a thin, glitzy dress that buttoned down the front. When she used the power steering, the dress twisted open between buttons, revealing a large black bra cup overflowing with Lenora. In the closed vehicle her mysterious scent was working on me as I confronted glossy pastel lips pressed together in an amused smile. This forty-year-old mother had morphed into a hot number, apparently for my benefit.

As dusk deepened into night she wheeled us around town in an aimless manner. Then without our having seen another store, she returned to the one where I worked and pulled into the alley behind it and killed the engine and lights. An incandescent bulb high on the building filled the Chrysler with brightness and shadow as my boss and I looked at each other. Her large blue liquid eyes seemed excited and expectant behind their oversized tinted lenses. "What are you thinking?" she asked me. As she knew well, I was thinking how nice it would be to start by kissing those delicious looking lips of hers. But I was also thinking how surprised her husband and daughter would be if they could see us together the way we were. I liked them both, especially the daughter, and felt I'd be betraying her if I had sex with her mother. What if we did it and my parents found out? Hardly an accomplishment to give them pride in their son! And if all that wasn't enough, I found Lenora's mature and confident sexuality somewhat daunting. Would I come up short with her and make a fool of myself?

I told her I was thinking about an upcoming math test that had me *very* worried. I inflated it into an improbable threat to my entire future. Her face fell a bit as she absorbed the unwelcome news she'd targeted her seduction on a dud. Then she wished me well on the test and thanked me for coming with her. We parted on good terms, I think. Anyway, I got the raise.

As I reentered the store trying to remember where I'd left my dust rag I noticed a change in Samuel. Opposite the downturned side of his mouth I saw half a smile, as though he remained generally gloomy but had found a ray of sunshine in having got the goods on his shelf duster. After that he was openly snide to me and doubled down on his brooding surveillance. I became convinced he wanted to catch me boosting something so he could report me to Lenora and get me canned. It wasn't pleasant working in that negative atmosphere and when a friend told me about a job with more hours at the fast food restaurant where he worked, I moved along. I recommended my buddy John Myer to Lenora as my replacement. Before John started I warned him to watch out for Samuel. "Something's wrong with that guy but I don't know what." I didn't bother to warn him about Lenora, figuring he could take care of himself with her.

John and Samuel happened to share a cynical outlook and soon became thick as thieves. Once Samuel trusted John enough, he revealed to him the dark goings on at the store. Apparently the chain owner, who was considerably older than Lenora, was involved with her in a long-term sexual affair conducted during working hours. The boss was paying her very well for her skill set while at the same time underpaying all his pharmacists, who to keep their jobs had to do double duty by managing their stores. This explained why Samuel was bitter—and probably also why he despised and distrusted me. He must have thought I was not only banging Lenora but spying for her. A boy toy management mole.

I wondered how Lenora had let herself become so morally

compromised. She was basically a prostitute conspiring to keep three coworkers performing her managerial duties for no pay. She was also cheating on her husband. Later, I realized her husband might have accepted his undistinguished role in the arrangement. After all, it boosted the family income, allowing them to afford an expensive second car and a big new house in a nice part of town. If love and trust are not what you seek in a mate, it can all make sense. But I don't think their daughter liked the deal. The sadness in her eyes came from somewhere.

FORTY-FOUR

N an East High hallway I was talking to one of the brighter members of the class ahead of mine when he changed the subject, saying, "I believe you know Lauren McCabe." His eyes were twinkling and he appeared on the verge of a big conspiratorial smile. I should have read the implications but his ambiguous statement caught me off guard and I answered truthfully, "She's my girlfriend." His smile evaporated as he realized I wasn't in on the joke but rather *was* the joke. Until that moment I think he'd respected me. He did his best to conceal his amusement yet in his eyes I detected a new sense of superiority based on the most fundamental one-upmanship. He understood he needed to explain his connection to Lauren, if only because I was tougher than him, so he said, "I met her at McDonald's. She mentioned she knew you." I didn't think the story ended there.

Lauren was proving to be a more popular girl than I could have hoped for. Even at my own high school she'd left her calling card—or cards. She seemed to be a standing joke and that made me wonder how many guys she'd been out with and how well they'd gotten to know her. I doubted she'd restricted them all to petting. I was beginning to see the downside of having a highly compliant girlfriend.

One night not long after, I was out cruising with a track team friend when I realized we were near Lauren's house. I decided to take him by so he could meet her. Her father came to the door and said she'd gone fishing with the boy across the street. "They'll be at the end of the peninsula," he added helpfully. He was referring to the spit of land between the Little Arkansas and Big Arkansas rivers at the place they merge, about a quarter mile from where we stood on the McCabe front porch. I'd never met Lauren's neighbor but she'd told me he worked at an aircraft plant so he wasn't really a "boy"— not to me. He was nineteen at least, and maybe older. The situation bothered me enough that I decided to drop in on the fisherpersons. I was feeling compromised in front of my friend and apparently thought I needed to prove something. Please don't ask me what.

Today that peninsula is a grassy, manicured acre on the grounds of the Mid-America All-Indian Center, but back then it was undeveloped municipal property covered in thick brush. A dirt path along the water's edge followed the contour of the peninsula and so did we, our course lighted by the glow of Wichita's nighttime business district not far downstream. I can't imagine what my buddy was thinking as I led our advance along that rut compacted by generations of fishermen. As we neared the end of the peninsula we slowed and moved quietly, sneaking in effect, and that's when the possible downside of my leap into action dawned on me.

I was taking us into what would be for me at least an untenable situation. If I caught the fishing party up to something, what did I plan to do—go Neanderthal? Not my style. It was even less my style to creep into position and spy on the action along with my teammate. Using my brain for once, I turned around and led us back the way we'd come. I felt humiliated but also relieved. I couldn't think of anything to say to my friend so I said nothing.

Lauren's friendships with the males of our city made me sad

but they didn't make me very jealous. The rage and agony that had filled me like lava when Katy merely flirted with another guy never arose with my second girlfriend though she gave me far more reason. I knew why. I didn't love Lauren as I had Katy, and since I didn't love her the things she did with other guys didn't bother me as much. Not to say I liked Lauren running around— definitely not—but I was finding I could accept it. I could accept it because Lauren and I made love almost anytime we could and she was an attractive and enthusiastic partner. I didn't want to give her up. What I found I *could* give up was my expectation for a relationship I took pride in. I began viewing Lauren as provisional and temporary, my girl for now. When I left for college in September I planned to let the separation end our relationship naturally and without hurt on either side. Until then I decided to follow Lauren's example by getting to know the girls of our city. If in the process I came across one I could love, I wouldn't need to feel guilty about it. Who would Lauren have to blame but herself?

FORTY-FIVE

N August of 1962 my family vacationed for a week in southern Missouri. We stayed in a cabin on a small hill overlooking an arm of water that meandered north from Bull Shoals
Lake. Fishing was poor the first couple of days we were there—
too much late summer heat under a cloudless sky—but the next
morning dawned cloudy and cool and I hoped we might do
better. Mom was frying bacon when my brother turned on our
portable radio for some music. Between country hits the DJ read
a news bulletin. During the night, out in Los Angeles, Marilyn
Monroe had died in her sleep. Her use of barbiturates was mentioned. Sounded like suicide.

The rest of my family seemed to take the news in stride, but
it bothered me. From my childhood I'd considered Marilyn the
most attractive of the Hollywood stars. I'd become a fan of hers
before I was old enough to see her films, knowing her from photos in magazines and from the Universal newsreels that played
in theaters. She always looked so completely alive, even in the
still shots. She combined the body type that will never go out
of style with a lightly modified face probably more exceptional
than Helen of Troy's. Her waif-like persona, a magnet for guys
with a protective streak, completed her triple whammy. Millions

of men were infatuated with her including a famous athlete and a famous writer, both of whom made the same foolish mistake. Women like Marilyn aren't meant for just one guy. They belong to the world and this one had the world at her feet. So why would she kill herself? Incomprehensible.

I forgot my plans to fish and pulled on my swim trunks. I walked down to our arm of the lake and went in, swimming till I got tired. Back on shore I was stripping water from my body when I noticed a girl in a one-piece standing on the other bank looking my way. Long hair hung dark and wet to her waist. Her face was indistinct because of the distance. Once she knew she had my attention she eased back her shoulders and posed her graceful, slim-legged figure. I was impressed—and not just by her shape. A girl so confident, I thought, would have a feisty take on things and be fun. She was about my age, surely no older. A girl older than seventeen wouldn't have been so demonstrative nor would she have been interested in me.

We looked at each other across the water for several minutes. I thought she wanted me to swim to her so we could meet. Maybe, like me, she was unsettled by Marilyn's death and was hoping to talk to somebody who felt the same way. I thought if I joined her she'd probably appreciate it and that we'd start off well. She was about a hundred yards away, an easy swim, though I knew a power boat might come bouncing up our arm from out of nowhere while its skipper drained a can of beer. That didn't seem likely however. Speedboats were whining out on the main lake but it was quiet where we were. Calm water mirrored tall cumulus clouds moving slowly through a blue summer sky. It was a landscape without people, except for us.

I was still debating whether to swim to her or not when she gave up on me. She turned her back and walked away up the hill on her side of the water. Her loose gait and the carefree way she swung her arms signaled I'd missed out on something good. She didn't look back as she continued uphill in her Keds to an asphalt road leading to a cluster of tourist cabins shaded by elms. As she disappeared under the trees I felt I'd let her down—that I'd let *us* down. But did I really? I still don't know what the right choice was.

FORTY-SIX

ON a September afternoon early in my senior year two of my East High classmates and I were riding around the city in a station wagon looking for action the way nerds typically do—with high hopes and low expectations. As we passed through a suburban neighborhood north of Twenty-First we noticed that a new ice cream parlor had opened and decided to try it. Inside were only three customers, all at one table, girls younger than us but not by much. They sat up straighter as we entered. Two were blonde and wore glasses. Both smiled at us, one revealing braces, the other a retainer. Mischievous nerdettes was my take on them. No doubt they'd detected in us the telltale markings of the male nerd and that's why we didn't in the least intimidate them, though we were older. I think we represented the action they'd been looking for.

The smile of the third girl was more subdued and she may or may not have been a nerd. She was definitely not blonde, nor bespectacled, nor dentally wired, nor in any way nerdy looking. She was dark and petite and so pretty I couldn't help staring at her. She reminded me of the girl at East I thought most attractive, our head cheerleader Jane Stevens, whose father's roots were Lebanese. Like Jane, this sophomore had olive skin and full lips.

Her chestnut hair was cut in a short bob and her earnest brown eyes looked right at me, making me think she might have a straightforward personality—something I'd been missing in my girlfriend. She seemed more interested in me than in my buddies, maybe because she could tell I was interested in her.

When a waitress approached and asked where we wanted to sit I pointed to the table closest to the girls. It must have been obvious to my friends that the dark-haired girl and I were connecting because they left me the chair next to her. Having been handed the perfect opportunity to talk to her, I couldn't think of anything to say. I was wracking my brain when John Myer broke the ice for everyone by asking the girls the obvious question, "Where do you guys go to school?" They were sophomores at East, excited about being in high school and by our interest in them.

The six of us left together, piling in one car "to save gas." John played chauffeur, with the blonde in braces next to him. In the backseat were Bob Nickel, the other blonde, myself, and the dark-haired girl, whose name I learned was Suzanne. She was as cute in profile as she was head on. She was about Katy's height but no doubt a few pounds heavier owing to her precocious curves. That evening she was quiet, letting her friends do the talking—which they were glad to do. One of them told us they were all daughters of machinists at Beech. Then we learned the girls were taking some of the honors classes John and Bob and I took as sophomores. That got the conversations rolling. I found it hard to pay attention though. My mind was on the girl beside me who seemed to be enjoying our cramped circumstances as much as I was. A happy mood amped by proximity prevailed in that wagon full of bright, witty teens.

John took a serpentine route through Wichita's northern and eastern suburbs then turned onto Douglas and drove west all the way into downtown. It was getting dark out, time for dinner with our families—but no one mentioned this. The evening was ripe with possibility and we were young and unconcerned with consequences, at least until we started home. John crossed the Arkansas River into our city's main municipal park and took us to the zoo, where he pulled into a small leaf-strewn parking lot next to the outdoor cages. Suzanne and I stayed in the car while the others got out and walked around looking at the few animals and birds still outdoors that late in the year. Most of the cages were empty. When I checked on our friends again, they'd all disappeared. Suzanne and I, who had begun to talk, stopped talking and began kissing.

Her lips were firmer than Katy's or Lauren's, and her kisses so dreamy I wondered where a sophomore had learned to kiss like that. Maybe it came naturally, I hoped. Her hair was soft and fragrant and she wore a quiet scent. Later, when I touched her breast though her sweater, she let my hand stay long enough for me to learn she was firm there too. She seemed to be made of less malleable flesh than other girls. We fooled around until our friends reappeared in a group, talking as they approached. It was time to go home, past time actually, yet John drove slowly back to the girls' car, extending our evening.

I didn't ask Suzanne for her phone number, believing she was too young to be my girlfriend. Ships passing in the night was how I saw us. After we sailed our separate ways, however, I kept remembering our time together. The strong impression she'd made on me stayed with me, to say the least. Although I barely knew her, her steady brown eyes made me think that if we ever had a long conversation it would go well. Maybe we'd be able to understand each other. Maybe she was looking for someone to be faithful to like I was. Such thoughts kept pestering me until I finally decided I might *not* be too old for her. Where there's love, I reasoned, the rest can be worked out. At that point I wanted to find her again, but how? Chances were slim I'd bump into her or her friends at East. Help arrived through John Myer, who I learned was dating the girl in braces. He said he'd try and get Suzanne's number for me.

While I was waiting, Rick Shafer dropped by my house one cold night with something to tell me. He looked a way I'd never seen him before—somber—so I knew the matter was important. He wouldn't divulge anything until we were alone. I told my parents we were going for a ride and soon Rick and I were speeding down a residential street in his Renault. Rick under normal circumstances viewed speed limits as suggestions, and he went himself one better on this night charged with madness.

"Can you get me a beer?" he asked. "They're behind your seat. Grab one for yourself while you're at it." I reached back and felt a paper sack containing two cold six-packs, one on top of the other. I pulled a couple of cans and opened Rick's for him. He took a long draw, issued a stupendous belch, then laid out the crisis. According to his contacts at West High, Lauren was dating another senior there, a name I didn't recognize. The romance had been going on long enough that their friends assumed they were a steady couple—as did Lauren's West High boyfriend apparently. Rick ended by saying, "I thought you'd want to know." Well, I did want to know, and I didn't want to know—and now I knew. I pulled two more beers.

Speeding nowhere in particular Rick bemoaned my unenviable state. He knew exactly how I felt because Lauren had done the same thing to him. A beer or two later he asked, "What are you going to do about it?" I told him I wasn't sure. He said, "If you want to talk to the guy, I know where he works." I wasn't yet drunk enough for that to sound like a good idea. Not until we were most of the way through the second six-pack did I grasp the compelling logic of showing up at my rival's job and starting a row. Rick, now with a destination, sped across town on Thirteenth. A few blocks beyond West Street he swung into the brilliantly lit parking lot of a supermarket and raced up and down the aisles looking for the guy's car. He skidded to a stop and pointed. "That's it."

My rival's love chariot was a 1955 Ford sedan—rechromed, shelled in countless coats of mint green acrylic lacquer, and in every way meticulously babied. Probably he adored the car. He even had the fuzzy oversized dice hanging from the rearview. What a dork, I told myself, *the dork who's fucking your girl!* I noticed that the Ford's baby moon hubcaps were glowing in sympathy with the blazing overhead lights. Maybe because they were so shiny those hubcaps focused my compromised attention. I stepped out of Rick's Renault and went to the pampered vehicle and looked it over. Yes indeed, the hubcaps more than anything else on that car recommended themselves as targets. I gave the one nearest the driver's door a swift kick, sinking a dent too small to be satisfying. I kicked again harder, then again and again, rising to a fury. I jackhammered that goddamn hubcap inward on itself beyond any hope of repair. Then I went to work on the baby moon behind it, bashing that one in. My demolition was making a lot of noise and as I put the finishing touches on hubcap number three several guys pushed through the front doors of the supermarket and walked fast in our direction. Rick jumped out of the car and stood beside me. I assessed our four opponents as they approached. Three were big guys. I figured we were in for it.

To my utter consternation, Lauren's West High boyfriend, by far the smallest of the four amigos, responded to my brutalization of his ride like a prince of pure reason. He was cool-headed, diplomatic, mature, well-spoken, and eminently likable—the very guy I'd pick to marry my sister, if I had a sister. With his beefy buddies standing behind him hankering to put dents in me, Mr. Cool apologized for dating Lauren and promised it wouldn't happen again. Smiling warmly he held out his hand and I meekly shook it. His gentlemanly response to my uncalled for violence undermined me so completely I craved his respect. I offered to replace the baby moons and went for my wallet to make a down payment. No, no, he insisted, his insurance would cover it. We were square in his books. He did think however that Rick and I might want to move along because his store manager had called the cops. That was probably a lie but my spiritual guide and I didn't hang around to find out.

This new low point in my relationship with Lauren offered the ideal opportunity for me to break up with her and date Suzanne. Yet when John got back to me with the phone number I knew I wouldn't call. My decision wasn't rational. A rational me would have dumped Lauren exactly as my West High rival had. With her surplus of guys she didn't need me on her team. However, as my passionate performance in the parking lot demonstrated, primal biology was overriding my reason. I'd gotten so used to having sex with Lauren any time I wanted that I'd turned myself into a buck driving rivals off his doe. On the night of the baby moons, without realizing what I was doing, I laid claim to Lauren publicly, branding her mine in the eyes of others and, more importantly, in my own eyes. Having made my choice, I let Suzanne slip into the past. Although this sophomore showed me I was looking for a girl I could respect and love, someone to fill my life the way Katy had, I let my libido lead me back to Lauren and her dependable gift of sex.

Lauren once told me she chose biology/physiology for her high school major as part of her career plan. She would continue her major in college, where she hoped to qualify as a tech in radiology. The end goal: a radiology job at a hospital. I pictured her at work as she rubbed shoulders with doctors and doctors in training. I knew some of them would be attracted to her. Was her real goal to meet and marry a doctor, I wondered.

I can't say exactly how, but I got the strong suspicion Lauren's mother was coaching her from behind the scenes. If I'd thought more about that, I might have realized a certain pre-law student had been added to the eligible physicians. Today I think Lauren and her mom were using the same technique to snare a husband that Mrs. McCabe had deployed a generation earlier to inveigle one of the most eligible young bachelors in Clayton, Nebraska into an unhappy union. Her strategy may have been handed down by her mother, who may have received it from her mother.

For the scheme to produce, one or more guys had to compete with the target for the same girl, triggering basic male instincts. Lauren's equal opportunity dating behavior seen in this light looks less like promiscuity than a way to keep me chasing her with blinders on. She and her mom were playing the game by the rules of the day, and skillfully. I was the inept one, several moves behind and oblivious.

Such courtship intrigue is no doubt rare today. Today a woman can have a career and make a good life for herself with or without a husband. But in 1963 most careers were closed to women and the surest route to prosperity usually lay with marriage to a prosperous man. It was an era of trapped men and women unfulfilled. We're all fortunate the old regime is now on its last legs, tottering into the sunset.

FORTY-SEVEN

BETWEEN dating Lauren and commuting to my new job as a window man at Sandy's I all but monopolized our family vehicle in the evenings and at night. Although no one complained, I began thinking I should get a car of my own to free up our family transport for others. In my own car I could pursue my budding semi-adult lifestyle more fully—an attractive prospect. When I began fantasizing about making love to Lauren in my own front seat, I *knew* I had to have a car. To pay for it I asked my night shift manager for as many hours as he could give me and he doubled my workload to nearly full time. On a hot Saturday afternoon in mid-September I went looking for my ride on the used car lots of my city.

For reasons now obscure to me, my friends and I had talked ourselves into a silly infatuation with European automobiles, especially European sports cars, so I had in mind to buy one of those. I soon discovered I couldn't afford a Porsche or Karmann Ghia in decent condition. In fact, within my price range I could find only one European car and it wasn't very sporty or even fully European. It was a Vauxhall or "English Ford," a smoke-gray sedan six years old with a fabulously waxed exterior. I climbed in and started it and to my delight the engine produced a highly appealing sound—as un-American as you can get. It didn't sound like a car engine at all, more like a lawnmower crossed with a vacuum cleaner. The foot pedal rubbers were brand new, telling me the car had received excellent care, and the lights and wipers worked superbly. The salesman wouldn't let me take it off the lot unless I had an adult with me so I went home and got my father. Only a few miles of test driving that sweet little gem convinced me to buy it, simply because it ran and was European, sort of. I made the down payment by selling my long-neglected coin collection. Dad had to cosign for the remaining debt because of my age.

A few days after my little gem came home its pleasant new car scent evaporated and the vehicle unleashed its underlying chemical stench. I investigated and found the engine block wet with brake fluid from the leaking fluid reservoir. This also explained the noxious white smoke that filled the car's cabin on longer trips. Fixing the leak, I discovered, would cost more than I could afford, so I began carrying rags to periodically wipe brake fluid off the block.

When the weather turned cold and the car wouldn't start in the mornings, I thought of the can of ether I'd found in the trunk. I learned to remove the air filter and spray the ether into the open carburetor, then hop in the car and fire the ignition. Three or four tries usually did it. If Lauren was with me to crank while I sprayed, one try could be enough.

The gas gauge was so hopelessly buggered that when the needle registered a quarter full the tank was dry as the Mojave. The air filter casing rattled at any speed because the wingnut designed to hold it down came loose on partially stripped threads. Sometimes the casing came off entirely and roamed around on top of the engine until I stopped, hunted down the wingnut in the street, and reattached the casing. The tubeless tires all lost air slowly but dependably and when one deflated below twenty pounds it could shuck its rim on any corner. Once I lost two tires on the same corner, presenting me with a logistical headache because I had only one spare. In the Vauxhall's trunk I carried an emergency kit in a cardboard box. It contained a hand air pump, a tire pressure gauge, several cans of brake fluid, two cans of ether, a one-gallon gas can, spare wingnuts, and a pile of rags soaked with brake fluid and oil waiting to combust.

My new schedule proved challenging. On weekdays after school I left for my job. Usually I got home around midnight. Often I'd be so jacked up from work I couldn't relax enough to fall asleep until two or three. Then up at seven for school. On nights I didn't work I usually saw Lauren and that kept me up late too. My first class each morning was analytic geometry and increasingly I couldn't muster the attention that course required. Sometimes my concentration drifted so low I nodded off. I fell behind and started cheating by copying a friend's homework. On tests my friend let me look over his shoulder. I learned nothing about analytic geometry and would have paid for it later had I gone on in math beyond high school, but I already knew I wouldn't.

Although I was a math major, I didn't see mathematics playing a significant role in my future. Being good in math I'd received encouragement to pursue it from the school bureaucrats, trying at that time to steer students like me into scientific careers so our country could defeat the Soviet menace. I didn't happen to share their fears. I thought the nuclear arms race was mankind's all-time greatest idiocy and wanted no part of it. Only if I'd had a deep interest in math would I have pursued it beyond high school. But other subjects interested me more.

In honors physics that fall I experienced a similar burnout. I remember the moment I lost my way. My teacher was explaining Torricelli's principle when my ingrained compulsion to keep up with twenty-five very bright minds was trumped by the realization that water spurting out of holes in a vertical pipe at different rates depending on hole elevation was not going to be important to me as an adult. Our classroom was on the third floor, slightly above the tarred and graveled roof of the East High gymnasium, and my attention would stray from physics to pigeons as they pecked in the gravel and wandered with apparent aimlessness among the huge steel exhaust vents. I learned those birds were merely faking nonchalance as they waited for the opportunity to mate in a vigorous beating of wings. I envied them, free and happy (I imagined), getting on with their lives as I wished I could get on with mine.

I wondered if anyone else in our class had had sex. I wondered if our teacher did it. I wondered if any of them could imagine what it was like having sex all the time. I didn't feel special exactly—but different, advanced. In this way I was already a man, getting on with my life. I spent much of that course watching the pigeons, staring at the clouds and daydreaming. I fantasized in particular about making love to Lauren, or about making love to Jeannie Veatch who'd sat behind me in English the year before. Trying to figure out how Jeannie's body so successfully combined oversized breasts and skinny legs reduced me to a happy dunce. While the rest of my class learned the basics of a science, I half dozed, useless as a buck lying in the shade with a hard-on. I absorbed just enough physics to get a B- for the semester—then dropped Honors Physics II which I was scheduled to take in the spring.

That whole academic year I gave minimal effort to my studies, lowering my class ranking from twelfth out of eight hundred to around twenty-third. Both parents were disappointed, and it couldn't have escaped them that my friend Bob Nickel held on to number one to become our class valedictorian. It was basically a lost year in my formal education as I devoted my time and energy to my *informal* education. With Lauren I learned the fundamentals of sex in a healthy, fun manner—giving me what I think was a solid foundation. At Sandy's I learned what a real job is like as I labored under an ambitious night manager who didn't believe in any worker ever coming to rest. We slaved every minute we were on duty, serving food, restocking supplies or cleaning up. If there was nothing else to do we polished the stainless steel counters and equipment with blue striped bar towels spritzed with carbonated water. Off the job, I learned the value of a dollar by calculating the cost of things I wanted to buy using the hours I'd have to work to pay for them. Even in school that year my informal education advanced. After I dropped physics I had two study halls a day to spend reading novels, a pursuit more important to my future than either math or physics.

FORTY-EIGHT

OR two weeks during autumn of 1962 the fate of life on our planet hung in the balance—or so history tells us. My clearest memory of the events comes from an evening in late October when I drove my friend Bob Malone to his house after school so we could do our physics homework together. Bob was the most gifted physics student in my honors physics class, and as we sat at his family's dining table discussing how to solve the first problem it didn't take him long to learn that my commitment to his favorite subject had gone AWOL. He was probably regretting having invited me to study with him when his father poked his head in the room to tell us President Kennedy was about to speak, in case we were interested. I was interested, Bob maybe less so.

We joined his parents and watched our President warn the Soviets that the United States was prepared to go to war if the Russian missiles armed with nuclear warheads weren't removed from their Cuban bases and shipped back to the motherland pretty damn quick. Kennedy also announced a naval blockade of Cuba to prevent new armaments being brought in. Some of the most frantic international diplomacy of all time happened in the days that followed. When the wheeling and the dealing were done, life on Earth continued, but the Kennedy brothers and Defense Secretary McNamara estimated that during low points in the negotiations the likelihood of nuclear war had stood at one chance in three. Since then, Russian leadership and our own have flirted with mutual self-destruction four or five more times—that we know of. Meanwhile other antagonists—India and Pakistan, China and the US, North Korea and you name it—have fostered newer nuclear standoffs, all making for a more dangerous world.

Weapons that exist nearly always get used. These particular weapons flying back and forth in a hot war among superpowers would likely extinguish life on Earth. It's why I've believed in nuclear disarmament since my teens. If we don't find a way to eliminate or severely curtail nukes, some year down the road while we're worrying about climate change or a new world pandemic, we'll bring Armageddon down on our heads through nuclear brinkmanship, misguided politics, miscalculation, or an angry wire up the keister of some robot.

I liked Bob Malone in high school and regret not seeing him at class reunions I've attended. Wondering what he was up to, I checked his personal information in my most recent reunion publication. Although he didn't give his occupation, I learned that the best physics student I knew in high school lives in Los Alamos, New Mexico. Los Alamos is where our nuclear weapons are designed. Bob could be breeding rabbits there, of course, but it seems more likely he continued his study of physics through college into a successful career, becoming one of the people who keep us armed to the teeth.

Bob and I have traveled far from that physics study session sixty years ago—diverging all the way. He apparently followed East High's STEM program into its highest reaches, where he is now a wizard. Meanwhile I dropped out and became an obstructive peacenik. The Bob I remember was not just smart. He was wise for his age—and a good person. I know he's thought carefully about what he does for a living and that he believes in it, though maybe with qualms. Probably he sees himself defending our country, and maybe he *is* defending our country. At some future reunion I hope my classmate and I get a chance to talk about where life has taken us.

FORTY-NINE

O N a frigid windless night early in January of 1963, when Lauren was eighteen and I was still seventeen, we'd been going at it in the front seat of my Vauxhall for half an hour and *I simply could not get there.* The near-zero temperature and the condom numbing contact with my partner held me back. Then all at once I could feel Lauren *mighty* well. Soon after, with a shiver of pleasure, I began firing—and my retreat was slow. Uh-oh, I thought. I reached down and found the condom hanging loose on its staff like a wet flag. A glance at Lauren's serene face told me she either hadn't noticed or wasn't worried about it. I remembered then that her period had ended only a few days earlier, and, according to the laws of physiology she'd explained to me, we were in the safe zone of her cycle. I relaxed and pushed the matter to the back of my mind.

My girlfriend was somewhat irregular, so when she missed her period in February she didn't give it much thought and neither did I. When she missed her period in March we did think about it, but Lauren drew on her knowledge of the female body to argue that she was almost certainly not pregnant. Just to make sure she went to see her family doctor and he ordered a "rabbit test," the technology of the day. She would get the results that

Saturday. We made a date to play tennis afterward, when she would give me the news.

On Saturday I picked her up at her house and drove us through a balmy late winter afternoon. Lauren guided me to a tiny city park in her neighborhood. It was an acre at most and contained two old tennis courts with sagging chain-link nets and fractured concrete. We made small talk in the car until I got tired of delaying the inevitable. I asked her if she was pregnant.

"Yes."

She did not want an abortion and I understood that. I could have pointed out that the honor of fatherhood might not be mine to claim, but I knew better. I remembered all too clearly dawdling in the breach with a torn condom—and the timing was impeccable. It was the most serious mistake I'd ever made and I knew I had to take responsibility for it. My first act as a man was to lift the pall that had settled over us. I said something like, "Guess we better get hitched before Pappy McCabe loads his twelve gauge." Lauren laughed, mostly from relief I'm sure. She seemed pleased I took the news well.

My equanimity was skin deep. Inside I was totally at sea, mind racing, adrenalin pumping, bowels quivering with misgivings and confusion. Lauren's pregnancy came as a shock because I was ridiculously unprepared. Her assurances she was *not* pregnant had allowed me to stick my head in the sand and hope for the best, blocking out undesirable thoughts. Now I was facing all those thoughts at once. Soon I would marry a girl I didn't love! I would become a father while still a teen! And I might have to skip college and work a factory job just to keep my kid in Pablum. What kind of future was that?

I thought tennis might take my mind off my troubles and help me relax, so we batted the ball back and forth for a while. Unfortunately, I couldn't concentrate on the game or calm down. My world was falling apart! How could I calm down?

After tennis it was late afternoon and we were both hungry. There was a burger takeout on Seneca two blocks from Lauren's house and she'd told me several times that her whole family liked the place. As we were passing it again she suggested we give it a try. We ate in the car and I was dismayed by the quality of the food. The hamburger meat had that going bad taste and the French fries were undercooked and slick with grease. While still eating I became nauseated. Lauren seemed to be enjoying her food and that worried me because soon I'd be eating her cooking. Why hadn't I noticed before that she couldn't taste?

I wanted to go home, be alone, and try to get my head around the situation. I planned to drop Lauren at her house. However, she had other plans. "Come in and say hi to my parents." Realizing Lauren's parents would soon become my parents-in-law, I followed my fiancée's wishes. We were climbing the porch steps when the aluminum storm door flew wide and Mrs. McCabe bustled forth onto the porch. Joy filled her face *and* her voice as she welcomed me like a war hero home from the front. I realized she'd been watching for us and that when she saw us coming up her sidewalk she knew I'd agreed to marry her daughter. She seized my bicep and ushered me into the house, then led me to the couch and sat me down. "We just finished supper but your dinners are warm in the oven. Are you ready to eat?"

"We already ate, Mom."

"At least have a piece of pie. I just baked it."

The TV was on and Lauren's cheerful older brother, whom I liked, was seated in a dining chair so far to the side of the screen he could barely see it. Lauren's dad was on the opposite side of the room in a more comfortable chair but almost as poorly situated for viewing as his son. Meanwhile, I'd been awarded the best seat in the house—the middle of the couch, directly facing the TV, with my queen to the left of me and the queen mother to my right. Clearly I was the guest of honor, even though I was perhaps the least enthusiastic bridegroom in Kansas.

The internal turmoil I'd been feeling since learning I'd be a daddy was now aggravated by a greasy gutbomb oversweetened with peach cobbler. The thermostat was set too high and so was the volume on the TV, perhaps to make it audible over Mrs. M's ringing enthusiasms. Her voice seemed to come at me from everywhere. It bounced off the walls and ceiling and reverberated in my skull. Under the duress of her happiness I was losing my bubble when in a dark flash of inspiration a plan for escape came to me. It would solve all my problems. To my troubled mind it seemed foolproof.

I departed not long after, waving good-by to a porch full of waving McCabes. My plan was in place and although I wasn't yet fully committed, it was winning me over. I saw nothing but pluses. I wouldn't have to tell my parents I knocked up my girl-friend. I wouldn't have to get married. And although there might be a baby, I wouldn't be the one grinding out a shift job at Cessna to support it. All these unwanted developments could be nipped in the bud.

I took the Seneca on-ramp to Kellogg eastbound. Once I was rolling on the throughway I held the speed limit until the lanes began rising for the river bridge. Then I floored it. My English Ford wheezed and popped, building speed slowly as it climbed the hump. From the bridge apex I took an affectionate last look at the Arkansas River, sliding south into the night, and felt a deep pang of regret. With the footfeed still pinned to the floor I barreled downhill, pulling away from the other cars. The stoplight at the bottom of the bridge turned green as I raced toward it. Then the two lights beyond it turned green together, as I knew they would. I will always remember those three lights lined up ahead of me, beckoning. Beyond them loomed the massive concrete abutment of the viaduct over the rail tracks.

My plan was now locked in. I was going seventy when I passed under the second light, eighty when I reached the third. With the end of my life closing fast it came to me why I couldn't do it. I could not pay my parents back for all their years of love and support by leaving them my mangled body to deal with. And I couldn't let the sum of my life be so small and so sad. I had to count for more than that.

Instead of steering into the abutment I held steady in the far right lane, streaking up the viaduct as I tapped the brakes. Already my mind was clearing of fog. From atop the overpass I looked out over the city, all the lights, all the people, and felt glad to be alive among them. Beyond the range of Mrs. McCabe's voice my future didn't look so abysmal. Yes, I would have a life a little different from my friends, but hadn't I always? I resigned myself to marriage and to becoming a father and drove home to find my family watching TV in the rec room—a touching scene for me that night. I joined them, glad I didn't have to cop to my screwup quite yet. I'd do it when my brother wasn't around.

The next day, given ample opportunity to cop, I did not cop. Same thing the day after. Soon the weekend was approaching and I hadn't told my parents and I hadn't called Lauren to ask her out. She must have thought I was ducking her. I was, but I had a reason. I'd reentered a state of denial and was hoping somewhat unrealistically that if I laid low and didn't make a move the problem would go away. After all, Lauren might miscarry. Or she might change her mind and give the baby up for adoption. Or one or both of us might be struck dead by spring lightning. A million things might happen. When I'd been hiding out for a week, Lauren's mother phoned my mother while I was at school and in hysterics described the dire predicament her daughter was facing all alone thanks to a certain young wild oat sower trying to abandon his crop. My parents were of course disappointed in me, very much so—I could see it in their faces—but they didn't punish me or even criticize. They left me to punish myself. I don't remember us ever talking about what had happened other than superficially. It had happened, so they busied themselves with the logistics of arranging a hurry-up marriage for a groom too young to marry on his own.

In late March of 1963 Lauren and I were wed by a justice of the peace in Newkirk, Oklahoma. That county seat promoted a sort of marital tourism by allowing brides and grooms to skip the waiting period required in Kansas. At lunch afterward the McCabes tried to make a glad day of it, reasonably enough, but the Harts rather ungallantly were not in the mood. Back home, Lauren concealed her pregnancy to prevent being kicked out of West High while I kept the marriage secret at East to stay on the track team.

FIFTY

OUR first track meet that spring was at Wichita South. I was seated on the infield grass doing stretches to warm up for my high hurdles final when teammate Steve Bradbury ran by, braces flashing as he shouted, "Jim's beating Charlie Harper! Jim's beating Charlie Harper!" Harper from Wichita North was the reigning Kansas state champion in the mile and Jim was Jim Ryun, a Wichita East sophomore competing in his first high school track meet. Surprisingly, Ryun did beat Harper that afternoon—a fitting beginning for the best American middle distance runner ever to put on spikes. Jim would go on to clock the first high school sub four-minute mile and compete in the 1964 Tokyo Olympics at age seventeen. In college he set a world record in the outdoor mile, then broke it, and set more world records in the indoor mile, the outdoor 1500 meters, and both the outdoor and indoor half mile. The summer after his junior year at KU, Jim silvered in the 1500 meters at the 1968 Mexico City Olympics.

Ryun's track career after 1968 brought more highlights, but his main accomplishments happened between ages sixteen and twenty-one—the years he and Coach Timmons functioned pretty much as one person with two pairs of legs. Most middle distance men don't reach full potential until their mid to late twenties, or even their thirties, making Ryun's meteoric rise as a teenager in track's most competitive event almost beyond belief. Sadly, Jim suffered a ton of mindless criticism for not winning gold in Mexico City as he'd been expected to do. I doubt he'd experienced significant disapproval earlier and it must have hit him hard. There was also an estrangement between him and Timmons that I learned about through one of our East High track managers who'd become a sportswriter. Based on what Don Stephens and I had seen, we both thought Jim was creating breathing room between himself and Coach to find out who he was as an individual. That would have helped him as a person, but it didn't seem to help him on the track.

Ryun was Timmons' coaching masterpiece and my teammate for a season. I remember him as a gangly, good-looking kid with a short, clean haircut. Toward me, his elder, he was friendly and respectful. He came to our high school to study at our vocational complex then got bumped onto college track because of his athletic skills. When he ran turns, in the beginning he rolled his head a little, striving for more power I think. It took Coach months to train that out of him and by then our best sophomore sprinter was rolling *his* head. After midseason, whenever Ryun competed in the mile Timmons provided splits by posting four guys with stopwatches around the track to shout interval times as he passed, keeping him on the chosen pace. Our familiar sports journalist from the Eagle-Beacon increasingly rubbed elbows with colleagues from out of town, drawn by the boy wonder. Jim was a really big deal—and we all knew it and I think we all approved. He worked three times as hard as anyone else. Why shouldn't he get the most attention?

President Kennedy had recently made the fifty-mile walk popular in America. When a local radio station sponsored Wichita's first fifty-mile competition, Jim ran instead of walking and won by miles. Years later, in a grocery parking lot near the KU campus, my former teammate and I crossed paths. We nodded to each other and exchanged warm smiles and I thought, same old Jim. Although I didn't know him well, I saw in him a sincere, kind, quiet guy. When in middle age he became a far right Republican congressman, I wondered if he'd been manipulated by people trying to capitalize on his fame.

My last year of track was, to be sure, less spectacular than Ryun's first year. I continued lowering my best high hurdle time as I'd done the two previous seasons and in every meet I made the finals. At the East High Invitational I won what we now call the Triple Jump. I had an advantage because I'd been practicing for months simply out of personal interest. At the city championships late in the season I placed fourth in the highs, and at regionals I took fourth again when two guys leading me fell down. Steve Bradbury pointed out that if only one more guy had fallen I'd have gone to State.

I accumulated more than enough meet points for a letter, but by the time I got my letter I'd graduated. Buying a letter jacket made no sense, so I put my big fuzzy blue and white W in my dresser drawer for safe keeping. Two decades later it disappeared during an estate sale.

There are many reasons Ryun's track career was more impressive than mine, but only one that concerns me here. Before meets, Coach Timmons would convene the team and ask each of us to declare a goal for our event. Most guys gave goals so lofty they sounded absurd to me, making me doubt the whole enterprise. When my turn came, I chose honesty over conformity. I trimmed a few tenths off my previous best high hurdle time and gave that as my goal—one I believed in because it seemed realistic. Timmons would be disappointed. He'd try to get me to lower my time to something I thought asinine. Wanting to please him, I'd do it, but I wouldn't believe in my goal. Once I got annoyed and piped up sarcastically with a goal a full second below my best, clearly impossible without a hurricane sweeping me forward. To my amazement, Coach missed the sarcasm and began glowing with that beatific mood we all knew well. He thought he'd finally got through to me. "Good, Hart!" he said. "That's the idea!"

I was the most difficult man on our team for the king of motivators to motivate—which is to say manipulate—and Ryun was the easiest. Jim was an average student from a working-class family and relatively unassertive. For these reasons I think he was unlikely to question authority in even minor ways. Meanwhile, I was a good student from a middle-class family who'd grown up questioning authority. I was so resistant to control I couldn't profit from what may have been Coach Timmons' most effective motivating technique.

FIFTY-ONE

DURING a visit to my hometown around 1970 I drove down Hydraulic Street for the first time in many years and learned the Alaskan Roller Rink had been replaced by an apartment complex with four two-story frame buildings, an outdoor pool, barbeque grills, and an expansive lawn. Attractive though the complex was, it made me sad. I pictured the jaws of a steel Tyrannosaurus rex biting into the rink dome and bringing away a mouthful of boards and hanging tarpaper. I saw hydraulic tusks submarining our vast tongue and groove floor and a grunting rhino grading the field where we played football into a dirt flattop ready for grass seed and equidistant saplings. The absence of what had been so real to me brought back my lost youth like a punch in the gut. Our magical rink, whose alchemy transformed lives, exists now only in photographs and in the memories of those she hosted under her high roof. With the Alaskan gone, I assumed the speed club must also be a thing of the past.

Late in the summer of 1972, five months after Lauren and I separated, our daughter Lynda, soon to be nine, visited me in Wichita. One day she asked to go roller skating. She'd heard her mother and me talk about our time at the Alaskan, and in Lawrence where she was living with Lauren she'd been skating at the local rink with her friends. I was flattered by her interest in something Lauren and I had devoted ourselves to and thought going skating with her was a fine idea. I'd noticed a new roller rink open on Kellogg not far from where my parents lived, so I drove us there. My daughter and I joined a free skate during a Saturday matinée just like those I'd known a decade earlier at the Alaskan. The same themed skates followed a very familiar sequence.

Lynda's economical style and good balance told me she was putting in the hours on her wheels. As a father it pleased me to imagine her with her friends doing something I knew was fun and healthy. She was a typical preteen in build—thin, straight hipped, and getting taller fast. Her brown hair, which had hung to her shoulders for most of her life, was longer now, parted in the middle and woven into two braids that lay on her chest in the manner of an Indian maiden or hippy chick. The color of her hair, her hazel eyes and the shape of her face resembled my own features closely enough that when we were together observant people could guess our relationship. She was an intelligent child apparently bearing up well in a new and more challenging home situation.

When the DJ announced Men Only, I got permission from my kid to see if the old man still had it. I was wearing my speed skates and the moves were ingrained so it didn't surprise me that I soon was flying past the session skaters just as in the days of yore. I was thinking I hadn't lost a stroke when I realized I'd picked up somebody on my tail. He was skating easily while I humped and pumped. I glanced back at a guy in his mid-twenties with a crew-cut and a familiar smile. He was an Alaskan racer from my time who'd been about twelve when I quit the speed club.

I looked around at the other fast skaters in the flow and saw Terry Pennick and several more who'd been on the club with me. Then I saw Coach Fite watching from behind the rail and knew our team had survived and found a new home. I thought Coach might not recognize me because in the decade since he'd last seen me I'd grown my hair into a mane and added a beard to my face. After Men Only I skated over to him with my daughter and introduced us, mentioning that Lynda was Lauren's kid too. Coach was polite but gave no indication he knew who Lauren was, though he'd once been her coach. He explained that the Hayes' had sold the Alaskan a few years earlier and moved their operations to the new location. Everyone was trying to keep things the way they'd been, as much as possible. After the matinée there would be men's speed club practice just as ten years before.

Coach and my former teammates were a little cool toward me and that was to be expected. We knew just by looking at each other that we stood on opposite sides of the cultural and political split dividing our country at that time. Our hair expressed the standoff. In the years we'd been apart theirs had remained short (from military style to rockabilly) while mine had flowered and gone to seed. The beatnik in their midst just happened to be the bastard who'd dropped the rink princess to date a girl who got around. I was curious about Katy, about what she was doing and who she was with, but I didn't feel comfortable asking them.

A few years later that new rink was demolished when the Highway 54 throughway swallowed its section of Kellogg—and the speed club lost its home again. Then I heard from Rick Shafer that a younger Alaskan teammate from our time, Maurice Swihart, had bought a rink in the suburbs out east and founded a new speed club there. Rick told me which members of our old group had joined Maurice's team, and although I can't remember even one of them now, I do remember that Katy was not among them. The next time I ran into Rick he said Maurice's venture had gone under. So far as I know the last vestiges of the Alaskan Speed Club passed into history with that business failure.

I'm not surprised that several of my Alaskan teammates later succeeded in other sports. The last time I saw David van Sickle he was top scorer on Southeast High's junior varsity basketball team. Odds are he went on to star for the varsity. Jimmy Brown joined the offensive backfield on West High's football team and was among the city's leading rushers his senior season. The last time we talked he'd been offered a college scholarship. Steve Bertholf became a standout long jumper at South High then attended Wichita State on a track scholarship. All those guys were Alaskan skaters close to me in age that I knew well. No doubt there were others before my time and after my time who contributed to our local sports scene. Several of the Alaskan girls would have excelled in high school athletics had such existed for them in those years before Title IX. I think of rangy Christine Moore who once sent two older male skaters to the emergency room from a tackle football game behind the rink.

During one of my visits to Wichita, and I can't remember when it was, Dad handed me two articles he'd clipped from the *Eagle-Beacon* and saved for me. One was so short I knew it came from a back page below the fold. It was strictly factual. At a rail crossing in a residential neighborhood not far north of my parents' house, two people in an automobile had been killed by a train in the wee hours of the morning. I'd driven through that elevated crossing many times and could picture the crash. The driver had tried to beat the train but didn't allow for the twenty-foot rise below the tracks. The names of the deceased were given along with their ages. I didn't recognize the man's name, but the woman was Charlotte Linsey. It looked like she'd partied right up until her last seconds on earth. Having lived her life to the hilt, she apparently died the same way, with apologies to no one.

The second article was longer and entirely upbeat. Our local business community had feted Katy Linsey as Wichita's new Secretary of the Year. Sounded like the Katy I knew. Same high competence and I'm sure the same high character. I noticed her last name hadn't changed. The reporter didn't go into her life beyond work and there was no photo. The piece was less informative than I would have liked but it did confirm my belief in Katy's abilities. I remembered the evening years earlier when our guidance counselor talked her into forgetting the career she'd dreamed of to train for secretarial work. By following his advice she'd become a standout secretary, but that didn't mean Mr. Sondergard was right. Someone with Katy's give-it-my-all personality likely wanted more challenge and more autonomy than most secretaries experience.

People say your first love is the one you can't forget. For me it's true. I remember my time with Katy as clearly as anything else in my life. Sometimes karma sends me by daydream, or by night dream, seductive fantasies of what might have been—dancing with Cinderella at the East High junior prom, walking with her down the aisle at graduation, losing our virginities to each other. I wish those had happened. They would have happened if I'd taken Luke's advice and been more patient with Katy about sex. As we less than omniscient beings negotiate life's choices guided by our own lights, most of us lose our innocence somewhere along the way. I lost mine at age sixteen when I dropped a girl I loved and who loved me to date a girl who gave me what I wanted.

A GENTLE REQUEST

Thank you for reading my book. If you enjoyed it and would like to contribute to its success, or just tell me what you think of it, please consider leaving a review on Amazon. Even a sentence or two would be a big help.

ACKNOWLEDGMENTS

Excerpts from this memoir appeared, usually in slightly altered form, in these publications:
Evening Street Review, chapter 22, titled "What Do You Want to Be?"
Under The Sun, chapter 4, titled "How I Made It to the Promised Land"
Wilderness House Literary Review, chapter 13, titled "Mother's Coronary"; chapter 40, titled "My Driving Teacher"; and chapter 43, titled "Boy Toy Management Mole"

I am grateful to the readers who provided thoughtful, constructive feedback on this manuscript as it became a book: my brother John Hart, who saw many of the scenes unfold, friend Victor Ortiz, classmates from Wichita East High School (Janet Harding, Jane Luellen, Connie McCune, Dan Millis, and David Willis), and members of Kathabela Wilson's Pasadena writers salon (Tim Callahan, Peggy Castro, Jackie Chou, Phyllis Collins, Pauli Dutton, Jim Haddad, Charles Harmon, Kris Kondo, Jonathan vos Post, Cindy Rinne, Sigrid Saradunn, Robert Stewart, Kathabela of course, and James Won). My most profound thank you goes to the editor of every draft, my most exacting, most helpful critic, my wife Jayasri.

Made in the USA
Las Vegas, NV
07 June 2021

24374758R00152